Tony Wilkinson was born in Doncaster, Yorkshire, in 1947, the son of a glassworker and a schoolteacher. He has been a reporter on BBC *Nationwide* since 1979. He was educated at Doncaster Grammar School and Leeds University, where he studied literature and art. He worked as a reporter on evening newspapers in Doncaster and Leicester, then, in 1972, he became a freelance radio reporter working mainly for the BBC in Leicester, Nottingham and Sheffield. He joined the *Today* programme on BBC Radio Four in 1976, working also as a foreign correspondent for radio stations in Africa and Australia. He transferred to *Nationwide* two and a half years later. He now lives in Bloomsbury, London.

Down and Out

Tony Wilkinson

Quartet Books
London Melbourne New York

Published by Quartet Books Limited 1981
A member of the Namara Group
27/29 Goodge Street, London W1P 1FD

Reprinted 1981

ISBN 0 7043 3366 X

Filmset, printed and bound in Great Britain by
Hazell, Watson & Viney Ltd, Aylesbury, Bucks

To Lindsay

Introduction

It was something new in television documentaries: a fictional character in a real world, a television reporter's eye in the body of an inarticulate derelict. BBC *Nationwide* reporter Tony Wilkinson became a down-and-out on the streets of London for a month to find out what it felt like to be at the bottom of the heap in Britain's Welfare State in the 1980s. For twenty-eight days and nights, the television cameras followed him as he took on the identity of an unemployed Yorkshire labourer, a fictional character whom he called Tony Crabbe. As Crabbe, he could win the confidence of the destitute and the authorities alike, and by arming himself with a plausible life history – one which, through research, he knew to be typical of the people he would meet – he could test how well the social workers and others found ways to help him. The cameras filmed him as he slept rough with chronic alcoholics under the Charing Cross Arches, they followed him into the flea-pit hostels and the squalid commercial hotels.

While the filming was going on, Wilkinson kept a secret diary on scraps of paper which he handed to a colleague every day to avoid reprisals from his fellow dossers and the authorities. This book is based on what he wrote, and on the tape-recordings made at the time. Many of the conversations are verbatim records, and their language is the raw talk of the streets rather than the novelist's highly wrought reconstruction of what might have been said.

Wilkinson's detailed record of his experience reveals a world which has changed little since the years of the Great Depression of the late 1920s and early 1930s when George Orwell underwent a similar ordeal on the streets of Paris and London. Fifty years on, the Welfare State had taken over many of the responsibilities of the charities in keeping the poor from starving, but it had done little to raise their spirits.

To his surprise, he found that the workhouse of Charles Dickens's day still existed – although now it was euphemistically called a Government Reception Centre. His experience at one of those centres – the Camberwell Spike – reveals how many of the staff consider it their duty to humiliate the poor to frighten them out of destitution. Wilkinson was forced to strip naked and undergo interrogation while he underwent a compulsory shower.

He endured the squalor and violence of Bruce House, a vast local-authority hostel where the staff padlocked the fire doors even though the drunks habitually smoked in bed. In a charity hostel, he was assaulted by a drunk on duty, a man claiming to be a member of staff. He slept on the floor alongside a prostitute who had just finished work for the night, and he narrowly missed a savage beating by a psychopath who chose as his victim a man only six beds further along the dormitory. He met a preacher who slept rough under the arches because he believed Jesus wanted him to be a tramp, and he witnessed the squalor of a commercial hotel which let chronic alcoholics stew in their own filth all day, sleeping off one drinking bout only to start the next.

After two weeks he dragged himself out of the mire, dressing himself in charity clothes and becoming a casual worker, one of the vast army of ragged men and women who are hired by the day to work in the heat of the kitchens of the best – and worst – hotels and restaurants in the capital city of the United Kingdom. He became a pot-washer at the May Fair Hotel off Berkeley Square, and at the hotel favoured by the world's most rich and famous people – Claridge's. He met Bernardo, a man who ate more good food than any of the wealthy guests, a sumptuous feast of leftovers that lasted from early morning until night.

The team which filmed him – cameraman Alex Hansen, sound recordist Brian Biffen, and director Mike Schooley – had from time to time to use the utmost secrecy to make sure they recorded the spontaneous reactions of the people he met. They used techniques never before attempted on a project of that scale. It meant that cameraman Hansen sometimes had to disguise himself as a down-and-out, concealing his £15,000 camera in a shoulder-bag while reporter Wilkinson carried a battered radio set with a concealed microphone built into it.

The preparation for the project had to be painstaking, too, to ensure Wilkinson's safety. His clothes were carefully selected and deliberately soiled to make sure he fitted the part exactly. Even the labels in the shirts had to be vetted. He was given a comprehensive medical which included a course of injections against the virulent infectious diseases he ran the risk of catching. Even so, he fell ill after only a week, and wandered the streets in a fever. But, like his fellow derelicts, he could not find a place to rest and recover, and doctors were reluctant to take him on their books because he had no fixed address.

He sought help from social workers, but found them of little use. A government welfare worker advised him to return to Yorkshire, even though there was less chance of finding work there although the advice ran directly contrary to government policy at the time.

He found it hard work being poor. On his budget of £4 a day, to cover board and lodging, he was hard-pressed to make ends meet. Without the daily routine of work, he was cast adrift in a world where the future barely existed, and where living through the day became an end in itself. Twice he was nearly arrested as a vagrant, and he felt himself becoming more and more isolated from the rest of society. The freedoms he expected from his irresponsible lifestyle never materialized. Life at the bottom was, if anything, more complex and harder work than his life as a sober and industrious citizen.

In the end, he was dismayed by the massive failure of the Welfare State to help the inadequates he met. Of even greater concern was the apparent inability of the politicians to recognize how, at a time when Britain faced its biggest recession since the 1930s, men who, through no fault of their own, found themselves out of work, risked dropping out of society altogether simply because they were lumped together with the derelicts and failures.

It was absurd; I was afraid of the streets outside my own home. After the months of preparation I found myself trembling at the thought of stepping outside. My hair had started to itch – it was still full of the brown powder and grease that had been applied by a make-up girl in the BBC studios. I looked out of the window; the street was quiet, an old man in a pork-pie hat wandered past the railings at the front. He looked drunk. How many times, I wondered, had I walked outside without a thought; what had there ever been to feel afraid of? Why should the streets seem any different to me now?

I looked at myself in the mirror. A one-day stubble was beginning to show, my hair had a crude bias to the left where the make-up girl had deliberately cut it badly; it fell in steps, and it was dirty, very dirty. It was all a game, after all; I was an actor about to play a part. I put on my hat, a woollen cap that had been trodden in the dirt the day before; and finally the big blue coat, the lining hanging from rents near the pockets at the front, the buttons missing, the carefully manufactured cigarette burns. It transformed me, I almost felt ashamed of myself. I put the coat back in the suitcase. It seemed too much like an actor's costume, and I had not even started playing the part. I would wear it later when I felt more confident in my role. Then I thought of the weeks ahead – it was not going to be like an actor taking to the stage for a few hours and then being able to return home to warmth and friends. I would be out there for a month. It was more like being a spy.

Suddenly, all thoughts of glory disappeared. It had been a bold gesture, a flourish in the radical tradition. Now I felt as though I had sold my soul. I thought about the weeks ahead when no one would want to know me, of the danger of living among drunks and misfits, of the possibility of arrest. In a flood of vanity I protested that I did not want to be this other person, this charmless inarticulate, this dosser.

The time had come. I gathered the radio with its hidden recording device and set off.

King's Cross Station was not busy at ten in the evening – a handful of people waiting for local trains, some bracing themselves for long journeys north. I sat on a low, hard seat facing the departure board, a small frightened man with a large white suitcase. I found my body adopting a posture of submission, of defeat, a slumping. I had no purpose, I was simply waiting for something to happen. A man with a briefcase sat beside me and began to read a magazine. A young couple embraced passionately a few yards away. I decided to buy a cup of tea from the buffet. I had been on the station less than half an hour, yet already time was heavy on me. I needed activity to punctuate the hours.

As I walked across the concourse I felt childish, exposed, as though everyone was watching me to see if I made a mistake. In the buffet, the queue wound around the counter two deep in places, so that newcomers had to squeeze past to reach the back of the line. A young student leaned away from me as I passed. To speak at all seemed an effort at first, I felt I would give myself away with each sentence. I knew I was being illogical, yet I imagined other people had a preconceived notion of who I was, how I talked. I felt I was taking part in an audition. A businessman viewed my heavily bandaged radio with distaste, as though I had carried infection into the room. I checked to see if the microphone was still switched on. I was in a hurry to record something now, something that might prove I had changed roles, as if by the act of recording I would bring about a change, a transformation in myself. I had reached the head of the queue. The girls behind the counter looked sorry for me in my dirty jacket and hat.

'A cup of tea, please,' I whispered.

'A what?' said a black woman.

'A cup of tea,' I repeated, trying to emphasize the northern u.

'Seventeen pence, darlin',' she said.

I was astonished at the price. I would not be able to pass the time by drinking tea, that was clear, or my daily budget of £4 would soon be exhausted. Why had I not noticed how expensive the tea was before I went into the buffet? I was still thinking like a man of means. I struggled with my suitcase and radio as I fumbled for more change; one of the girls sighed with impatience. I could sense people in the queue behind me shifting uneasily. I gave the girl 20 pence, and while I was waiting for the change, I tried to place a plastic lid on my cup to keep the tea inside warm. It took longer than the time to fetch the change from the till. Two men behind me looked at each other in exasperation.

I carried my cup outside into the station concourse. I was glad to get out of the buffet, the proximity of so many other people had made me feel claustrophobic. In the open air I was less noticeable. I resumed my seat in front of the departure board; the lovers were still in passionate embrace and a man in a sheepskin coat was finishing his cup of tea, tilting the beaker high in the air to catch the last dregs. He tossed the empty cup carelessly over his shoulder, letting it fall among the rest of the debris scattered on the floor. I was strangely angry. I wanted him to set a better example, to live up to his standard of dress. I smiled at the absurdity of my reasoning; I was going out of my way to feel morally superior.

The tea felt wonderfully hot against my throat, and I gulped it down, anxious for the sensation of warmth inside. Yet, only an hour before, I had been sitting at home, relaxing after a big meal. The Last Supper. I began to remember it course by course, wondering when I would eat as well again. To my astonishment, I found myself shivering, yet the air was not cold. I had begun to adopt the physical symptoms of my role. I finished my tea and walked towards the trains. A few passengers were boarding a diesel bound for a local destination. They slammed the carriage doors behind them. I began to feel that a station was the worst place for someone in my position in real life; there were too many reminders that other people had places to go and reasons for travel.

Two hours. I had been on the station for two hours, doing nothing, going nowhere. There was a waiting room on the far platform. Inside, a man wearing a sports jacket and trousers was stretched out as if he were lying on a chaise-longue, his head propped against his arm, back to the wall. I sat opposite him, on a long, mock-leather bench seat. He seemed to be wide-awake, watching, afraid to let his eyelids droop. Unlike me, he had no luggage, not even a plastic carrier-bag. For ten minutes neither of us moved. I wondered how long the waiting room stayed open, whether I would be able to sit there in the warm all night. From behind a partition I could hear the sound of snoring; in the dog-leg of the room, other people were lying full-length on the benches, asleep.

It was long after midnight, and I decided to lie down too. I was afraid I would lose my radio if I fell asleep, and I placed it under my head as a pillow. At first, I tried to keep my eyes open. The man on the chaise-longue stared directly at me, his head still propped against his arm. How long had he been lying in that position, I wondered. Was he a traveller waiting for a train, or someone like me, just passing the time? He seemed to be waiting for something to happen. I closed my eyes, hoping to sleep until it did. A sudden feeling of panic came over me as I shut off my vision of the room. How would I know if someone were to attack me or try to steal my radio? This was a public place and I was totally unprotected. I opened my eyelids a fraction so that I would still look as though I was sleeping. I glanced around. The man opposite continued to stare, but he did not move. For twenty minutes I continued to pretend I was asleep, holding tight on to my radio, just in case. Then I closed my eyes at last. I wondered what might happen if I was found by the police; would I be arrested? How would I be treated? I began to feel my heart beating, and I half-opened my eyes once more. Still no move-ment. I thought: perhaps they would let me stay here all night. I tried to remember what they could charge me with if I were arrested. Vagrancy – was there such a charge? What if I were to tell them that I had been waiting for a train. Obstruction, then. I supposed they could always charge me with that. But who or what would I have been obstructing? Waiting rooms, after all, were provided for the purpose of waiting. My problem was that I was not waiting for anything in particular. There was the sound of a door opening. I half-opened my eyes; the man opposite had gone. Had whatever he had been waiting for arrived? I heard a voice from the dog-leg.

'Come on, come on.'

My heart beat faster. Was this the police? What would they do? The voice was louder.

'Are you travelling?'

The question was for me. I opened my eyes and saw a policeman's uniform. The buttons seemed very bright.

'What can I get you for?' he said. 'Are you travelling, are you going anywhere . . .?'

I grunted.

'. . . or are you just using this as a hostel?'

'I was having a sleep,' I said. 'I . . .' I began to get up.

'Sorry, mate,' said the policeman. 'For the travelling public.'

'What do I do then?' I said, trying to subdue my speech to appear as humble as possible. My heart beat even faster.

'What do you do? Well, go and see the social services in the morning. But I'm afraid members of the public complain about people sleeping in here. OK?'

I stood up and began to collect my things.

'Sorry about that,' he said, and he turned away to see if the other sleepers were following my example. Both uniformed men began to shake a well-dressed youth whom I had seen entering the waiting room about an hour before. He had seemed respectable and in control; I had assumed he was a genuine traveller. Now he lay there inert, apparently unconscious.

'Come on, mate,' said the other policeman. 'For the travelling public.'

I approached the policeman who had woken me and asked him if he knew of anywhere I could go.

'Have you got any money?' he said.

'Not . . . no . . .'

'No?'

'Well, I've got a quid or so, but that's about it.'

'Where are you from?' he asked.

'Doncaster.' I told him the story I had worked out in advance, that I was an unemployed labourer who had come to London looking for work thirteen months before.

'Were you like this when you came down?' he said, looking hard at my torn and filthy car-coat.

'No, I were . . .'

'You were clean, and had a job?'

'Yeah.'

'Well,' he said, 'you've seen the other scats on the station, haven't you?'

'The other what?' I said.

'Itinerants. You'll be like them in two years if you stay down here.'

'Well, what do you suggest I do, I mean . . .'

'I suggest, in the final analysis, you go back to Doncaster.'

'Well, what do I do tonight?'

'Tonight, you can't stay here. There's no hostel that I know of. Just have a walk round, come back in the station later on. But as far as sleeping in here, you can't sleep in here. There's fare-paying passengers and it's not fair on them, OK? Walk round, come back on the station, have a coffee, sit on the bench, you might get moved on again . . . all right?'

'All right, ta.'

I began to walk towards the door. A small, frenzied man had entered the waiting room and seemed to have been listening to our conversation. He asked me if I had anywhere to sleep. I told him I had just been moved on for sleeping in the waiting room, and I had no money. The policeman repeated his view that I should travel north to Doncaster.

The small man said: 'You'd be better off up there . . .'

'But I haven't got any money,' I said, wondering who the small man was.

'You could get a travel warrant, perhaps someone up north can lend you some money,' said the policeman. 'As I say, you'll be a vagrant within two years, and you're too young for that, aren't you?'

The small man said: 'If you've got no experience, you'll not get a job down here, he's not having you on. I found it hard to get a job, and I've got experience.'

I thought: experience of what? Who was this man, and what was his interest in me?'

'And this lot,' said the policeman, pointing to my radio and my suitcase, 'you'll get it nicked, eventually.'

The small man told me he might be able to get me a bed for the night. He said he had been working all night and he was tired, so he would not be able to take me there himself. He would make a phone call to make sure everything was all right.

'Who are you?' I asked.

'Simon Community,' he said. 'We try and help the people who are out on the streets. We've got houses.' His accent was sociological cockney, an educated man trying to sound less educated. He took me to a telephone kiosk.

'I'll see if I can fix you up with them, if they'll have you,' he said. 'It's up to you whether you go or not. It's either that or get lifted.'

There was someone on the other end of the line.

'Hello?' he said. 'Is that Frances? Ah, Tom here, Frances, King's Cross. Listen, you couldn't do us a favour, could you? Listen, I just ran into a copper on King's Cross, right? There's a lad down here, out. And if he doesn't get put up for at least a night, they're going to lift him . . . Yeah, sorry about that, Frances, but they're going to lift the bloke, you know. Somehow he's trying to find a way that he can get back up north. You know, the copper's told him if he hangs round here they'll lift him. If I explain the way to get there you'll accept him? Hang on, I'll give you his name.' He turned to me. 'What's your name?'

'Tony Crabbe,' I said, sticking to the surname I had chosen for my fictional identity.

'Tony Crabbe,' he said, 'his name is Tony Crabbe. OK? Yeah. OK, thanks very much, France. 'Bye.'

He put the phone down, then he said: 'You've got a roof over your head. I'll show you how to get there.'

We sat by the buffet, which had long since closed. The lights were out save a few behind the counter, and the staff had all gone home. It was 1.30. The man from the Simon Community drew a map showing me how to get to a house with a black door, which he said was about a quarter of an hour's walk away. The map was very crude, and he tore up his first attempt and tried

17

again. Once more, he apologized for not being able to take me there.

'I wish I could,' he said, 'but I'm knackered.'

He gave me a note to hand to the girl he had spoken to on the telephone. We said good-bye, and I walked out of the station, suitcase in hand, towards the derelict hinterland beside the railway lines.

The map was so badly drawn I had little idea of its scale. Only one street was named – St Pancras Way – and there were references to post office delivery vans and a pub. A hundred yards down the street, I stopped to look again at the map. I could make out what looked like a railway bridge, and I wondered if it could be the one immediately ahead. I looked up, and in the shadows just before the bridge I could see two youths standing by a derelict house. One spoke softly to the other, looking towards me. Muggers, I thought. I must have seemed an easy target, a simpleton with a suitcase and a radio, and there were two of them. I looked around. Two men were walking up the street in my direction. I waited till they passed, then followed close behind. As I drew level with the two youths in the shadows, one of them moved forward, but his friend held him back, nodding towards the two men. Perhaps they were policemen, he seemed to say. I was safely past.

No. 50 St Pancras Way was a once-respectable middle-manager's house backing on to the Grand Union Canal in the no-man's-land behind St Pancras Station. It formed part of a block of half a dozen Edwardian houses which were now separated from a once-prosperous street. I rang the bell. The black door opened a few inches, and a girl's face peered through the gap.

'Hello,' I said. 'I've got this note.'

'Are you Tony?' she said.

'Yeah.'

The door opened wider.

'Oh, come in, love, we've been waiting for you. You took your time, didn't you?'

She seemed to be in her middle twenties, a frail girl in a long skirt. There was something old-fashioned about the way she dressed – like a hippie from ten years before. She led me along a dimly lit corridor, past a curtain hanging in a doorway. There was a smell of stale sweat, and I could hear someone snoring.

'Are you trying to get back up north?' said the girl, looking concerned. Her front teeth stuck out, giving her face a permanent smile.

'Yeah,' I said, 'but I've got no money.'

She showed me into a kitchen at the back of the house. A kitten brushed against my leg. By the sink, a man was lying full-length on the floor, covered by a blanket. He was awake, and talking to two other men, one of whom was drinking a cup of tea. The girl introduced me by name, and I nodded towards them, trying my best to look confused and frightened. I was obviously over-acting.

'You look all in,' said the girl. 'Put that case in the front room. I'll show you where you're going to sleep.'

We went back down the corridor where a bench seat and two chairs stood against the wall like furniture in a doctor's waiting room. The girl pulled back the curtain in the doorway and pointed to a space on the floor. I could see men lying side by side across the full width of the room, covered by blankets. They were like the wounded from a recent battle. A man's feet hung over the end of a sofa. The girl slid my suitcase into a corner, and pointed once more to the space at the foot of the sofa.

'You can squeeze in down there,' she said. 'OK?'

I nodded. There was barely enough room for me to lie, and I would have to be careful not to wake the others. We returned to the kitchen.

'Have you eaten?' said the girl.

I did not reply. What could I say, I who had eaten a big farewell dinner only a few hours before?

'I bet you haven't had anything since this morning,' she said. 'Don't worry, we'll find you something.'

She looked in the oven and pulled out a plate containing a meat and potato pie, sprouts and chips.

'Who's this for?' she asked the three men. They all shook their heads.

'Right,' she said, scraping the food into a frying pan, 'wash this dish and we'll warm it all up.' One of the men rinsed the dish with boiling water from a big old kettle which had been steaming on the hob. The girl heated the food thoroughly and then transferred it on to the dish. She added two cold sausage rolls for good measure.

'There,' she said, handing me the dish. 'That should fill you up. Just go and sit in the corridor on the bench there, and help yourself.'

She fetched me some salt and brown sauce to add to the flavour. I ate a few mouthfuls quickly, while she was still watching, then I slowed down. I had already begun to feel bloated. The kitten that had followed us into the kitchen when we arrived watched me from the stairs. I slowly swallowed a sprout. The cat licked its lips. Half an hour later, I had eaten most of the food, but a sausage roll and a few chips remained in the bottom of the dish.

'Don't worry,' said the girl as she came to collect my plate. 'The cat will love you.'

The kitten followed her into the kitchen, crying loudly for food. I followed too.

'Have you got a job?' said the girl.

'Not at the moment,' I said. 'I used to do a bit of painting and decorating, like.'

'Oh,' said the girl, 'we might be able to get you a bit of work through one of our other places.'

She gave me a blanket and a candlewick bedspread, and told me to make myself as comfortable as possible in the other room. I pulled back the curtain, and laid the bedspread on the floor, doubled up, to form a thin mattress. I put my radio to one end as a pillow and lay down slowly, avoiding two pairs of feet sticking out from blankets to my right. I decided to keep my clothes on, including my shoes and jacket.

In the half-light, I counted another nine people in this end of the room, five of us on the floor. The far end of the room seemed to be a dining area, and I could hear more snoring from there, too. At my feet, by the curtain, a man was sitting in an armchair, smoking. His legs and knees were covered by a blanket, and he seemed to be watching me as I settled down for the night. I turned towards the sofa and shut my eyes. The blanket smelt foul. Someone in the far corner of the room farted noisily. The two men nearest to me were snoring. The smell of sweat was overpowering at first, but I found it less objectionable after half an hour. I became aware of stockinged feet only a few inches from my head. It meant that I would not be able to turn over in my sleep without coming into direct contact with them.

I found it difficult to sleep at first; the floor seemed hard and the farting and snoring continued to disturb me. After an hour I became aware of something pushing against the back of my head, a series of short, sharp thrusts. I turned and saw a man's foot snaking towards me, covered by a foul woollen sock. At such close range the smell was bitter, and I pinched the foot to make it go away. There was no response. I wondered if the man was awake and if this was some kind of territorial claim, keeping the newcomer in his place. I pinched the foot again; this time it moved to one side, and I settled back to sleep. It seemed only a few minutes later that I became aware of someone stepping over me. There were voices, and I saw what I thought to be a boy's face above me. He looked very young, I put him at no more than fifteen or sixteen. His face seemed very smooth. I could hear Frances, the girl who had shown me in, giving whispered instructions. I looked at my watch under the blanket. It was three o'clock. The boy settled himself at right-angles to me, head-to-head. He covered himself in his blankets and fell asleep within a few minutes. I marvelled at his apparent sense of security while I lay gripping my radio against the thieves of the night. The next time I woke it was morning.

> 'It may be winter outside,
> But it's spring in my heart.'

It was a girl's voice, singing loud and full in the far corner of the room. I looked up and saw a man adjusting the controls of a large radiogram. A thin grey light struggled through the window on to the sea of sleeping men. The man in the chair was awake, and smoking. He had a pointed beard, like Leon Trotsky's. A disc-jockey's voice on the radio told us that there had been a frost during the night, and that today would be cold.

'Glad I wasn't out last fucking night, then,' said the smoker.

I looked at my watch. It was seven o'clock. I felt stiff, my right hip ached. I could make out a noticeboard on the wall above the mantelpiece; the rest of the room seemed sparsely furnished. A gas fire, a threadbare carpet, two sofas and three armchairs. All the furniture looked as if it had been bought in the cheapest of second-hand shops. The black vinyl sofa that I had been lying beside had given way in the middle, the underside touching the floor. It divided the front room from the back – someone had knocked down the partition wall to make one big room.

'*Tat-tat-tat-tat-tat-tat!*' A man wearing a pork-pie hat and a lumberjacket began to make sounds like a child imitating machine-gun fire from the other side of the sofa.

'The battle of fucking Anzio beaches,' he said.

'More like the fucking Battle of Gettysburg, that,' said another man who had joined him. They were both looking at the bodies lying on the floor.

I turned to the boy who had arrived at three o'clock that morning. He was still asleep, a half-smile on his lips. There was something almost feminine about his face. Then I noticed that he was wearing false teeth. It was not a boy after all, but a woman, elfin-faced, in her early thirties. Who was she, I wondered, and why had she arrived so late?

'If I'd known she was here,' said a red-haired man on the sofa under the window, 'I'd have been on top of that last night.' He laughed.

Frances was in the hallway, helping a grizzled old man to put on his boots. They seemed too small for his feet, and his face was screwed up with concentration.

I got up and went into the kitchen. The 'trusty' who had switched on the radiogram told me to help myself to bacon and eggs.

'Do I have to pay?' I asked.

'No,' he said, amazed that I should even think of payment.

There were three or four other men in the kitchen, buttering bread, boiling eggs, frying bacon. One of them was an old man who wore a tight-fitting sweater tucked inside a pair of outsized suit trousers – which were held up with braces. His hair and beard were the palest grey, his skin bloodless, so that he looked like the corpse of an old sea captain. I looked at his feet – he wore open-toed sandals, even though the temperature outside hovered only a few degrees above freezing-point. I took some bread and margarine into the dining room. A notice on the door said 'Diner's Club Cards Welcome'.

The man on the sofa by the window was still stretching as I helped myself to marmalade. He began to discuss murder with the man in the pork-pie hat, a subject they both obviously relished.

'Shepherd's Bush is the worst,' said the man on the sofa, 'it's wicked.'

'Good place to get mugged, is Shepherd's Bush,' said Pork Pie.

'Mind you, there's a fucking good pub there – Fullers and Youngs.'

'I saw a bloke in Shepherd's Bush, a dosser, with his throat cut from here to here,' said the man on the sofa, drawing a line with his finger from ear to ear. 'He'd been mugged,' he added.

I was amazed by their conversation because Shepherd's Bush was where I worked, and it had never occurred to me to be afraid there.

'There's been a lot of people killed in Shepherd's Bush in the last year,' said the man with the Trotsky beard. 'Mind you, there's a lot died from the cold too.'

I sipped my tea. Through the back window I could see washing hanging on a line. I walked out into the yard, where I found piles of old clothes in boxes and plastic bags. I washed up my breakfast plate and cup. In the corner of the kitchen was a door leading to a bathroom, and I went inside. I found a bath, hand-basin and toilet, and underneath the window an automatic washing machine full of clothes. That was where the shirts had come from hanging on the line outside, I thought.

I returned to the front room; only two people were still lying on the floor, and I found a space to sit on the end of the black vinyl sofa.

'How much did you pay for that bottle of cider yesterday?' said Pork Pie to the man with the Trotsky beard.

'A fucking pound,' he said.

'It only costs seventy-five pence a bottle, dunnit?'

'Yeah, we was fucking done.'

Pork Pie looked at a notice on the board above the mantelpiece. 'You call this writing, George?' he shouted. 'No one can make fucking head nor tail of that. You're fucking illiterate, George.'

I gained the impression that he was making sure we knew that he could both read and write. A mongrel dog ran into the room, and Pork Pie found a ball and began to play catch.

'Come on, Dosser. Dosser!'

The dog caught the ball in its mouth. Pork Pie hid the ball behind his back, and the dog chased after it, leaping over the man and the woman still asleep on the floor. The game woke them up, and they struggled to their feet. The woman wore black, shapeless trousers and a thick, ribbed sweater. Her clothes were neat, but not designed to attract men. Frances sat down near me on the sofa and called everyone to the breakfast meeting. A dark-haired youth was put in charge of the minutes; he sat in a corner on one of the armchairs, a clipboard on his knee. Pork Pie chattered on about the police, claiming he had been picked up the night before by the Special Patrol Group.

'All I was carrying was this load of plates and some plastic bags,' he said.

'Well, what did you fucking expect?' said a man in the dark corner of the room near the window. 'They always pick you up if you've got a bag late at night.'

'Do you mind?' said Frances. 'We're trying to start the meeting.'

'Yeah, well, hurry up, will you?' said Pork Pie, karate punching the air. 'I've got a job this morning.'

'Let's start with yesterday,' said Frances, looking round the room.

'What did you do yesterday?' said Clipboard, looking at me.

'I was picked up by the police at King's Cross,' I said. 'Someone told me to come here.'

'That'll do,' said Frances, 'you've no need to go into any detail, it's not an interrogation.'

She told Clipboard to write down, 'King's Cross, arrived 3 a.m.'.

The questioning switched to someone else. The man with the

Trotsky beard said he had been on Hampstead Heath. He did not explain what he had been doing there, but later he told me he had been sleeping rough. 'I've got the whole kit,' he told me, 'blankets and the lot, and I always keep a change of clothes in a poly bag. I needed them, too, we got soaked in that storm. That's why I'm in here.'

It was the girl's turn. She said she had been working until three in the morning and had come straight round. She did not specify the work, but a few days later I saw her with other prostitutes plying for trade outside King's Cross Station. I was surprised that she looked so plain, so middle-class. She seemed to hide her sexuality rather than display it. But her smile was pleasant enough, the smile of the plain schoolgirl who cannot afford to be as awkward as her prettier pals. Frances said she would fix her up with a dental appointment later that day.

Many of the others said they had been looking for work or walking about. Someone asked Frances if there was somewhere more permanent to stay, and she described a Simon Community farm in Kent. She said Clipboard had stayed there once, and had enjoyed it very much.

We moved on to the next section of the meeting: plans for today.

Pork Pie said he was going to work; the man who had slept on Hampstead Heath said he was going for a drink; and I said I was going to look for a job.

'Does anyone fancy going to the pictures tonight?' said Frances.

She suggested we might all go and see *Breaking Glass*. Those who could afford to pay, she said, would have to find the money themselves, the rest would be paid for – at least, in part. Hampstead Heath said he was not sure if *Breaking Glass* was to everyone's taste. Not everyone liked pop music, he said, whereas the film *McVicar*, about an escaped criminal, was probably much more suitable. He sounded like a councillor in a committee meeting. Frances said they would decide on the film later.

Everyone was allotted tasks. I volunteered to sweep the back yard and clean the outside lavatory. Others said they would peel potatoes or clean the stairs or sweep the hallway. No one was allowed to remain idle.

Later I was called to the upstairs office. Frances asked me to sit down. It was a scruffy room with posters, drawings and poems pinned to the walls, and a large desk under the window. One of the poems read:

> There was a young girl called Lily,
> Who went for a walk up the Dilly,
> A charming young flirt
> Put his hand up her skirt,
> She said don't stop that feels quite thrilly.

Frances asked me what I planned to do in the next few days. I said I would like to look for work, and if possible stay another night on the floor in the front room.

'Well,' she said, 'you really need a proper bed, especially if you're looking for work.'

She thought for a few seconds, then she said: 'We may try and get you into a hostel in Hammersmith called Riverside, but even they only allow people to stay for three weeks. Still, it's better than sleeping on the floor.'

She said she would talk to some of her friends while I was out about accommodation and the possibility of work. In the meantime, she said, I had better come back that evening.

I thanked her, and left the office, surprised that she had asked me no questions about money. For all she knew, I might have been entitled to enough state benefit to afford my own flat, yet she had not asked if I was even claiming any money.

Alone, in the street I felt a sudden elation. I was free of my role as Tony Crabbe, if only for a few hours. I walked quickly down the street, anxious to leave behind the people who knew me only in my fictional role. I wanted desperately to speak to someone who knew me as myself, as if I might lose touch with that sense of self if I did not reinforce it. There was a telephone box on the corner; I opened the door, looking around as I did so in case I had been followed. It was ludicrous that I should even contemplate such cloak and dagger manoeuvres, yet I feared discovery every moment, discovery which I imagined would prevent my continuing as a down-and-out altogether.

Even speaking to the operator on the telephone was an intense pleasure. I had been playing the part of Tony Crabbe for only twelve hours, yet I had felt an urgent need to hear the sound of my normal voice. I used charm by the yard, it was a proof that I still had a middle-class persuasiveness, a plausible manner, even if I could only use it when the person I was speaking to could not see me. It was too early to get a reply from my office, and I began to telephone friends and colleagues, reversing the charges, to tell them how I was getting on. I recounted conversations, gave descriptions, wallowed in anecdote like a cheap guest on a TV chat-show. I revelled in being able to tell jokes about myself, alarming some of my friends by my jollity. They told me later I had sounded as if I was on drugs. Most wanted to know how I had survived the night in the cold, and seemed a little disappointed that I had found shelter. I gained the distinct impression that they thought I had been cheating.

As soon as I left the phone booth, a depression settled on me. I was alone again with my new role. People in the street looked at me with contempt. I felt I could approach no one, not even to ask the time of day. I was more isolated than I could remember ever having felt before. A motorist stopped his car by a parking meter and fumbled in his pocket for change. He turned to me and asked if I could change a pound note. I saw his eyes dart downwards to my filthy shirt and torn jacket.

'Oh,' he said, putting the pound away, 'sorry.'

I found a public gardens next to a junior school. The sound of children's laughter rang clear against the high-rise flats. After a few minutes I began to feel better. I was not having to be Tony Crabbe at all, sitting in the sunshine watching the day go by. I was just a man on a park bench. No one expected anything of me, I had no need to pretend to be anything.

The autumn sky was clear-blue, and the sun felt warm on my face. I watched a little Asian girl sitting cross-legged on the playground, her hands over her eyes, counting. Around her, other children scattered and hid. None of them noticed me, and I was grateful. To their teachers I must have looked dangerous, perverted. The sound of the children's voices made me think of the days when I had played truant at school. Yes, that was it, I was playing truant. I felt guilty, a sense of having avoided something I should have done, and finding myself with more time on my hands than I wanted. I had never been a persistent truant for that very reason, my sense of boredom and guilt always overcame my sense of pleasure at having avoided something nasty. I was already beginning to feel bored. How would I fill in the hours between now and evening when I returned to the Simon Community?

Two girls passed by my park bench. They were in their late teens or early twenties. I smiled, and they quickened their pace. So that was another loss I would have to come to terms with, I thought – my loss of sexuality. I could look forward to being regarded as dangerous, or, at best, someone *hors de combat*, a neuter.

I set off for the city centre, walking down back streets I had never noticed before. I found shops selling the most exotic specialist products, a purveyor of accessories for whippets, a theatrical hat suppliers, a pornographic book exchange on a market stall. It seemed to me an underworld hidden from general shoppers.

On the main streets I was more despised than I had noticed before. I felt people were willing me to step off the pavement to let them pass. They walked round me as if they were avoiding dog faeces. I looked in the shop windows of Regent's Street with new eyes. With no money, shops became curiosities, places where other people bought goods, and I relished the eccentricities of the window displays rather than their relevance to me. In an expensive menswear shop near Savile Row, I caught a shop assistant glaring at me through the window as I admired the haughty expression of a dummy wearing riding clothes.

My budget was £4 a day – a little less than my fellow derelicts received on Supplementary Benefit, but I would not be spending much money on drink. I looked at the menus in cafés to see what I could afford. Most of the prices were too high for me to buy anything more than a starter, and, in any case, I was too poorly dressed even to contemplate going inside.

I had been advised by the BBC doctor to concentrate on high-carbohydrate foods like fish and chips to give me enough energy to combat the cold. It looked, anyway, as if such foods were all I would be able to afford.

I found a fish-and-chip shop near St Pancras Station. The owner was a small, harassed Cypriot with a ferocious wife. As I was about to pay, she shouted: 'Is he eating here or taking it out?'

The intensity of her voice caused her husband to drop 5 pence on to my plate in surprise. I felt angry. She had assumed that I was trying to cheat the shop out of money. That my honesty could be called so easily into question because I looked poor seemed to me totally unreasonable, and I glared at the woman.

'It's OK,' said her husband. 'He's paid for eating inside.'

He leaned towards me and apologized for dropping the 5 pence piece which was still lost among the chips.

'Be careful not to swallow it,' he said.

I wandered round the shops all that afternoon, but the curiosity I had felt at first began to fade. Shops were places for buying things, and I would not be able to do that for another four weeks.

By late afternoon the contempt from passers-by began to depress me considerably. It was no use telling myself that I did not deserve such looks of loathing, and that my personality was still intact under the dirty surface. Knowing that I had weeks of such contumely to follow, I began to hate the person I had become for visiting hatred upon me. It was his fault I was despised, his fault I was denied human warmth, and I wanted to murder him then and there. If only I could tell people who I really was, I thought, they would understand. But there was no way I could approach people. I felt a pressure to conform as strong as anything I had experienced since being a teenager, the claustrophobic feeling that acceptability was only a change of clothes away.

I recalled that I had felt little sympathy with beggars who had approached me in the street. The Welfare State was meant to have protected me from such people. No one had a need to starve, no one had a need to beg. Now that I was on the receiving end, all this seemed so much theory. It was me who was being ignored, me who was abused, and I felt the weight of a great injustice. I tried to say: I am human like you. But my appearance only succeeded in communicating: danger, do not approach. It was like a radar signal being jammed.

I had my first hamburger that evening. With a glass of milk it cost me 84 pence – though I had to pretend that I was taking it out of the shop to avoid paying VAT. After my experience in the fish-and-chip shop that lunchtime, I could see no reason why I should not cheat a little, if that was what people expected me to do.

It was ten in the evening when I returned to the black door in St Pancras Way, long after the daytime callers had finished their free soup and bread and disappeared into the night. The man who answered the bell seemed reluctant to let me in; his face was unfamiliar, aggressive.

'How do you mean, you've come to stay?' he said. 'You stayed here last night, did you?'

'Yeah.'

'And were you told to come back?' he asked.

'Yeah . . .' I said.

'Who did you see?'

'France.'

'Frances? Hold on there, I'll ask her.'

He left me in the hallway while he went upstairs to the office. I could hear the sound of a television in the front room; a show-jumping competition was in progress. A cultivated voice said: 'He's done it, David Edgar has done it, a splendid clear round.'

The aggressive man returned. There was something military about his manner.

'You'll be all right,' he said, and he disappeared into the kitchen.

I pushed aside the curtain leading to the front room, and placed my suitcase in the corner. I recognized the clipboard monitor in the far corner, and the trusty who had helped me get breakfast that morning.

'We've just been to the pictures for an hour,' said the Trusty.

'*The Shining*,' said Clipboard. 'He's a great actor, Jack Nicholson. It were all about this old hotel, and he's got this axe. It was great.'

Clipboard seemed vague about the plot, he could only remember fragmentary details.

'They stuck this axe right in him, right in here,' he said,

pointing towards his stomach. 'It was a chef at the hotel, like. He got killed by mistake.'

'And he must be delighted with that performance from so young a horse,' said the show-jumping commentator on the television. The voice sounded smug and upper-class in a room so bare. The makeshift curtains dangled precariously from a loose rail above the front window, threatening to fall off and veil the show-jumpers in yards of cheap floral print.

The Trusty asked me if I had had any luck in finding work that day. I was surprised he had remembered.

'I might have something in a couple of month,' I said.

'What are you going to do till then?' he asked.

'I dunno,' I said.

He looked at the television. 'Isn't it a quarter past, yet?' he said. 'What's happened to *Kojak*?'

The prostitute who had slept next to me on the floor the previous night came in, and began a soft conversation with the Trusty. She seemed to be making some sort of arrangement with him. She was dressed differently from the night before, a well-cut denim coat, smart jeans and expensive leather boots. She picked up a copy of the *Sun* and turned to the television page.

'It says *Kojak*'s at seventeen minutes past,' she said.

'Great,' said Clipboard.

She went into the corner and picked up a pair of dark-grey trousers from behind the chair. They looked like the ones she had been wearing the night before.

'Whose are those?' said an Irish youth with a short haircut.

'Mine,' she said, as if it was no business of his.

She went over to the Trusty again, and whispered something. Then she turned to leave.

'I'll see you, then,' she said.

Kojak was just starting, and the five people in the room began to shuffle in their seats in anticipation. On the armrest of the black vinyl sofa, I found a copy of a comic-strip book which the Irishman had just put down. It was a war story with a square-jawed hero who had been badly treated because he did not come from the right social class. He was a sergeant who should have been an officer, but who had been discriminated against by the British class system.

'It's only because his dad didn't go to a posh school that he failed the officers' training course,' said a private under his command.

The sergeant got his chance when his superior officer was killed in battle. In frame after frame, he was seen leading his men to victory against ape-faced German troops.

'You die, Englander,' said a man in a German helmet.

'Take that, Fritz,' said the sergeant, hitting him squarely in the face with a rifle-butt.

'Lumme,' said a private afterwards, 'no one could have led us better than that.'

'He only failed his officers' training course because he was said to lack the qualities of leadership,' said a brigadier. 'By George, no one could say that about him today.'

Kojak had started. The villain was an American version of Raffles, an improbable high-class burglar who had fooled the police for years with his brilliant escapes.

'That's Manalito,' said Clipboard, 'from the *High Chaparral*. He's a great actor.'

I watched the faces of the men in the room as the story progressed. They seemed to identify more with the anti-hero than with Kojak himself. The villain was portrayed as a master of his craft, a kind of gymnastic chess-player who was eventually allowed to escape with the loot. There was an audible sigh of relief as he made his getaway.

The Trusty said: 'Has it started? Fucking hell, I must have fallen asleep.'

The Night Man, who had answered the door to me, switched off the television and distributed blankets for the night. There were far fewer people than the twenty or so who had stayed the previous night, and only two of us had to share the floor. The man who had slept on Hampstead Heath took the settee under the front window, the other sofa was occupied by a barnacle-faced old man with bad feet. I watched as he struggled for some thirty minutes, trying to remove his second boot. The foot seemed to have swollen, causing the laces to draw tight. I was allowed three cushions from the armchairs to lay on the floor. They made a narrow but comfortable bed. An old Irishman whose coat looked even more torn than the one I had in my suitcase was to sleep on the floor beside me, but he said he preferred to lie on the carpet. He had a cushion only for his head. I smelt the acrid odour of sweat once more as I pulled the blankets over my face, the smell of scores of sleepless nights. I wondered if I would ever get used to that stink. I could feel the dying warmth of the gas fire on my back as I turned over to sleep.

At four o'clock in the morning I heard a voice from the next room.

'We'll take my racing car,' it said, 'it's got the power for the job.' There was a pause, then the voice said: 'Sixty thousand pounds.'

It was a conversation with an imaginary person, a dream about power and money, with the sleep-talker the man who made the decisions.

'No, I think Europe,' he said. There was another pause. 'All right, twenty thousand, but not a penny more.'

It sounded like a bad TV script with a cool hero and money-no-object. The one-sided dialogue continued for another ten minutes, never making real sense. Hampstead Heath on the sofa farted, loud and long. I felt cold, and reached down for my bedding. All but the candlewick bedspread had fallen to the floor.

At seven in the morning the Irishman got up and hurriedly readied himself to leave. He had only removed his shoes when he had gone to bed. He tied the laces, and put the seat cushion back in the armchair. A few minutes later I heard him chiding someone in the kitchen for failing to wake him earlier. I wondered what appointment he could have been so anxious to keep.

The Night Man switched on the radiogram. Capital Radio. He had difficulty in adjusting the volume. The set was so old that it went loud or soft unpredictably, like a deaf old man. I folded my malodorous blankets into neat squares and laid them beside the heap that the old Irishman had left on the floor. I wondered if anyone might think my neatness inconsistent with my personal habits. After all, my appearance was not that of a punctilious man. I looked around, no one seemed to notice. In the kitchen, the Trusty was busy already and in a mood to give orders.

33

'Make a pot of tea,' he commanded, 'and when it's ready, take it into the dining room. The milk's in that jug, and the sugar's over there.'

I obeyed, anxious to appear humble and willing to please. I was like a child looking for house points at school. As I hurried to and fro, the Trusty kept his eye on me, pointing out the things I had done wrong, telling me where I could find crockery and cutlery. He seemed to be adopting a fatherly role, showing me the ropes, yet, at the same time, keeping me in my place. I tried to complete my tasks as quickly as possible, and when I had done as he said, I asked if I might boil myself an egg. He said that would be all right, but he disapproved of the method I tried to adopt – putting the egg into a pan of cold water.

'Not like that,' he said, grabbing the pan and removing the egg. 'You should always put the egg into the pan when the water's boiling, then wait three minutes.'

I nodded, humbly. When my egg was cooked I looked around for a teaspoon to eat it with.

'There aren't any,' he said.

I took the egg, together with some bread and margarine, into the dining room. There were dessert spoons already laid on the table, and I used one to prise the top off my egg and scoop out the contents. It was my third free meal at the Simon Community, and I wondered whom I had to thank for such generosity. Was this a religious charity, I wondered. I looked around. There was a crucifix on the dining-room wall, but no other outward sign. No one had mentioned religion – so far. I poured myself a cup of tea. The disc-jockey on Capital Radio said: 'You're looking lovely this morning, no bags under the eyes I'm glad to see.' I felt less than lovely.

In the corner of the dining room sat an old man with a character actor's face, like a batman who had seen better days. His crumpled white shirt was open to the navel, where it followed the contours of his huge belly; around his neck was a stylish, if dirty, cravat.

'Nearly as good as the Britannia Club in here,' he said. His voice sounded like a butler's.

'You mean the Britannia Club in Singapore,' said someone

34

from the far shadows of the room, 'the naval club?' There was no hint of irony in the voice.

After breakfast the Batman recalled a meal he had enjoyed at the Britannia Club. 'Pretty splendid rissoles, if I say so myself,' he said. 'A touch more seasoning might not have gone amiss, but they were pretty damn good.' He emptied an ashtray into a pedal bin, an ostentatious display of tidiness in front of Frances and another, red-haired woman. I saw their eyes follow his action, then look away. He examined the ashtray to see if there was any remaining debris, and finding a residue of fine ash, he glanced around to see if anyone who counted was watching, and he flicked it behind the bin with a deft movement of the wrist.

It was nine o'clock when the breakfast meeting began – about half an hour later than the day before. The Night Man was in command, the square-jawed sergeant who would have been an officer if only his dad had gone to a posh school.

'Come on, come on, breakfast meeting,' he said. 'Let's get a move on, we're late.' He glanced round nervously, to see if anyone was listening. Slowly, a group gathered in the front room.

'Come on, hurry up,' said the Night Man, his pen poised over the clipboard. 'Are we all ready? Right, yesterday. What did you do yesterday, Willie?'

Willie was a tall, gaunt, gormless youth who looked back to front. His belly protruded, but he seemed to have no buttocks at all. He seemed to be racking his brain, like a contestant in a quiz show. Then he forgot the question.

'What did you do yesterday, Willie?' repeated the Night Man with more patience than I had expected. Willie looked at the wall again, searching for the answer. His hair was fashionably close-cropped, and he wore expensive-looking dark glasses. I had met pop musicians whose appearance was not dissimilar.

'I went to . . .' There was a long pause. 'I went to . . .' Another long pause.

'Where did you go, Willie?'

'To Victoria . . . no, to Charing Cross.' He seemed relieved. Then, another question.

'What did you do there?'

It was almost brutal to test his memory further.

'I . . . I . . .' There was another strained intermission, then Willie said: 'I had a cup of tea . . . and I . . . went for a walk.'

The Night Man began to scribble: 'Went for a walk near Charing Cross.' Then he looked up, and pointed towards the man who had slept on Hampstead Heath.

'I peeled a ton of spuds in that fucking kitchen, didn't I?' he said. 'Then I went down the benefit office to get some money, but they weren't wearing it.'

The Night Man again scribbled on his pad. His writing seemed very slow and deliberate. He pointed at me.

'I went to West Hampstead to see this bloke about a job,' I said. 'He said he might have something for me in a couple of month.'

He wrote: 'Looked for work.'

Clipboard said he had been to the housing department to ask about rehousing. He added that his name might be appearing in the next edition of the local paper, because he was going to speak to a reporter about it. Other than that, he said, he had been to the cinema to see *The Shining* and he had watched the telly.

There were only two men left. The Trusty said he had prepared food all day, and the old man with the barnacled face said he had arrived in the afternoon. He did not say from where. I was curious to know the purpose of these questions and answers. They seemed so cursory as to be without value, unless it was to give us some sense of order and achievement. We moved on to our plans for today.

'I'm going down to Camden Press,' said Clipboard, 'so watch out for my name in the paper tomorrow.'

Frances joined us. Her presence seemed to unsettle the Night Man who began to display all the symptoms of someone under threat.

'Bloody hell, Frances,' he said, 'we'd nearly finished when you came, now we'll have to go back to the beginning.'

'Why?' said Frances.

'Because we haven't done you. What did you do yesterday?'

'I got up at seven,' she said. 'I worked in the office . . . I went to the cinema . . . and I watched the news on telly.' She sounded as hesitant as the rest of us, as though she wanted to be mistaken for a resident rather than someone official and infallible. She was wearing the same skirt and jumper as the day before, and her feet were bare.

My task that day was to help the Trusty prepare food for the day visitors – a vegetable soup made in a huge pan. He felt the need to teach me everything, including how to peel potatoes with a blunt table knife.

'Just take them like that, and get the skin off them,' he said, sculpting a potato into a complex geometrical shape.

'Who's it for?' I asked.

'What, the soup? For homeless people; you know, people like you, fellas that have been sleeping rough. We sometimes get as many as two hundred coming in here during the day, and they all need feeding. They sit on the benches in the hallway.'

We prepared several pounds of Brussels sprouts. The Trusty showed me how to cut off the ends where the stalks had turned brown. I washed up the plates and dishes as we went along, and he showed me where to put them on the shelves. It became obvious that he was treating me as a kind of apprentice, someone he expected to stay for some time.

At ten o'clock I went up to the office to see Frances. The red-haired woman was there too, a dowdy woman in her thirties whom I had thought to be another prostitute. I had heard her asking where the nearest launderette was, and I assumed that she was using the Simon Community as a temporary base. The Trusty had told me she was his 'boss', and she was all right. I had not realized that he meant it literally.

'I know I look as though I'm one of the inmates,' she said, 'but I'm actually in charge of this place.' She and Frances asked me if I had found the job I had been looking for the previous day. I told them I had been half-promised a job in two months' time.

'Well,' said the House Mother, 'that's not much use for now. What are you going to do for money?'

'I don't know,' I said. I wanted her to ask me more questions about money, but she shied off the subject as if she were afraid to pry.

'What do you want to do now?' she asked.

'I just want somewhere to sleep while I look for work,' I said.

'Well, it's difficult to get you into a hostel at week-ends, they're all full. Do you need some time to get your head together?'

'No,' I said, 'I just want to find a job.'

She did not look as though she believed me, and she said: 'I think the best thing is if you stay here over the week-end, then we'll try to get you somewhere better. How long have you been in London?'

'About thirteen month.'

'And have you been working?'

'Well, I've been staying with this mate rent-free, while we've been converting his house,' I said. 'When we'd done it up, like, he kicked me out.'

The House Mother looked at Frances as though she had heard similar tales before. I told them I had been staying in bed-and-breakfast accommodation since then, until my money ran out. The two women talked briefly together, but neither asked me if I had claimed any state benefit. The House Mother turned to me again.

'You look a bit rough,' she said, 'and you'll have to clean yourself up if you're going to get work. Have you got a razor?'

'Yeah,' I said. 'Can I use the bathroom then?'

'Yes, of course,' she said, 'and we'll try and get you some better clothes. We'll get Jim from the other house to show you where to go. All the clothes are at No. 129. He'll take you. He's a bit slow in starting in the morning, but he'll be here later.'

I went down to the bathroom and shaved, lathering my face with ordinary soap. It had been several years since I had used a safety razor, and I had to be very careful not to cut my face. From the other side of the door I could hear several people complaining about the length of time I was occupying the bathroom.

Jim arrived half an hour later; he was the Irishman with the short hair I had seen with the comic book the night before. I explained to him that I needed new clothes, and I asked him to show me where to go. His answer was almost unintelligible. It was a speech pattern which formed itself into clusters of staccato followed by long stretched words made more complex by a dense Irishness of accent.

We set off for No. 129, he dressed in smart jeans, with shiny black shoes and a checked sports coat only one size too large, I in my oil-stained car-coat and dirty woollen hat, carrying my suitcase.

'You can leave that here,' said Jim, pointing to the case.

'No,' I said, 'I'll take it with me in case I want to keep some of the clothes I've got.' It was a lie. I was intending to abscond from the Simon Community as soon as I had my new clothes.

'Well,' he said, 'it's quite a walk, so leave it if you want.' We set off at breakneck speed, he marching more than walking, always one pace ahead. He looked like a country boy in the city streets, a fresh-faced youth with a public-school haircut, striding out for Camden Town. I had put six pound notes down my sock before we set off, to make sure I still had them with me if I changed jackets. I could feel them beginning to chafe as we marched along, they seemed to be rising up my leg. The suitcase, too, was uncomfortable, too heavy for the speed we were going, and I swung it in rhythm with my feet. After some fifteen minutes, mostly in silence, Jim stopped suddenly outside a large Edwardian terraced house. In the small concreted garden at the front was a dustbin, on top of which was a black suitcase similar in size and structure to my own. Jim examined it closely, trying the catches. One was broken.

'I'll pick that up on the way back,' he said.

No. 129 Malden Road was a decaying turn-of-the-century mansion with a stepped portico leading down to the street. A haggard old woman was leaning against one of the plastered columns by the door. She watched us closely as we passed, like a sentry. I made my way to a dingy back room where a plump-cheeked girl was standing by a desk.

'I was wondering if you'd got any clothes,' I said.

'Yes, yes, of course,' she replied. She was very tall. I could imagine her playing hockey. She led Jim and me into a narrow room next door, a giant clothes cupboard of a room, lined on both sides with jackets, trousers, shirts and ties. The floor was deep in clouts which had been tried on and abandoned.

'What's your shirt size?' said the girl, crouching among a pile of loose clothes at the back.

'Fifteen,' I said, beginning to sort through the jackets on the racks. I found a full evening suit with a shiny shawl collar and a double stripe down the trousers. I was tempted to try it on just for the hell of it. Perhaps, I thought, I would be able to get a job as a waiter. There was a dark suit which looked as though it had hardly been worn. I tried on the jacket; it was made for a man almost twice my weight – the shoulders drooped down my arms, the sleeves covered my hands.

'Try this one,' said the girl, handing me a smart checked shirt.

I took off my own filthy shirt and vest, much to her and Jim's distaste, and I tried the shirt on. It was a perfect fit.

'Great,' I said, and I tried on a sports jacket. It was slightly on the small side, but it would do.

The girl looked pleased. Jim, in the meantime, was trying on jacket after jacket, finding it difficult to keep his balance on the pile of clothes. Trousers, I thought. I needed some trousers to replace the badly holed pair I was wearing. I tried on a pair of salmon-pink jeans.

'You can go down into the bathroom in the basement if you want,' said the girl, embarrassed. Jim stared at me as though I was mad.

'No, I'm all right,' I said, struggling to pull the jeans higher.

They were obviously made for someone very much smaller than me. I took them off and tried on a pair of suit trousers. The waistband billowed like a sail. I tried on three or four more likely pairs, all too big or too small, until finally I found a pair only slightly too short.

'These'll do,' I said, 'if I can pin them up. There's no button at the top.'

The girl gave me a safety pin, and I pulled the tops of the trousers together. They were also slightly too small. Jim, who had found himself a blazer, burst out laughing. He was amazed at my lack of embarrassment, and he clearly found my behaviour beyond the pale.

I put my old clothes in my suitcase, thanked the girl for her help and set off. In the daylight, Jim's new blazer looked crumpled and old, far worse than the garment he had arrived in. There was a curious tide-mark running round the back of the collar. On the way back, he picked up the black suitcase from the dustbin.

The occupants of the house sat in the window, watching him examine it, wondering what he was going to do. I motioned to them, asking if it was all right to take it. A studious-looking woman said yes, it was all right; she mouthed the words silently through the window. We walked on to a park, where Jim opened the suitcase and emptied the contents into a litter-bin. There was a pair of child's wellington boots, and carrier-bags stuffed with old pens and books. It seemed strange to be sifting through other people's belongings in this way, the objects seemed too private, too personal for us to be throwing them away so callously. I began to wonder about my own clothes too. Who had worn this jacket and this shirt before me? What had happened to them now, were they alive or dead? I felt in the pocket of my jacket, and pulled out several nuts and bolts and pieces of silver paper rolled up in balls. I shuddered. I felt as though I had been grave-robbing and I was now sorting through the spoils.

We set off again, Jim once more marching a pace ahead. I could not help thinking what a comic pair we must seem, both in ill-fitting second-hand clothes, both carrying large suitcases. The money I had hidden in my sock began to work its way higher and higher up my sock, until it was in danger of falling out. I stopped and transferred it to the inside pocket of my new jacket. As I bent down, the zip on my trouser fly gave way, and I tried to button my jacket to hide the sight of my shirt-tails. But there were no buttons on the jacket, and I was forced to hold it to with my free hand. The length of my trousers seemed to be causing some amusement to passers-by. With my undersized jacket and my half-mast trousers, I looked as though I had been standing out in the rain. I asked Jim where the nearest benefit office was, telling him I had to call in to claim some money. He said there was one on the way to the hostel, in St Pancras Way, and he would show me where it was.

We arrived there some ten minutes later. A sign outside said the building was a branch office of the Department of Employment, and I told Jim not to wait, since I might be some time. He nodded, and bustled down the road, suitcase in hand. I went to the entrance marked 'B' and walked inside. There was a poster on the wall urging me to consider retraining. I waited a few moments, then cautiously looked outside to make sure Jim had gone. Then I took my suitcase in hand once more and walked briskly to a near-by pub. I telephoned the film crew. My involvement with the Simon Community was over, and I was free to graze fresh wastelands.

The pub was not a fashionable one; it had a huge semi-circular bar, all brass and wood like the stern of a river-boat. The landlord was telling a lonely overweight man a few home-truths about women, a subject he seemed to regard as one he possessed a good deal of expertise in.

'I've told you which pub,' he said. 'The point is, there's music, and all kinds of women, divorcees, young ones, middle-aged ones, virgins. You can't bloody fail.'

'Don't listen to him,' said a barmaid hurrying in from a back room. 'He knows nothing about love.'

'Who said anything about love?' said the landlord. 'We're talking about the basic drive, you know, like dogs.' He came over to me.

'Are you leaving town?' he said, looking at my suitcase.

'No,' I said, 'I'm staying.' He smiled, and served me a half-pint of bitter. I was pleasantly surprised by his attitude; for the first time in two days I had experienced none of the repulsion which I was beginning to take as normality. The new shirt and jacket seemed to be doing the trick, especially since I had a clean-shaven face to match. I stayed for half an hour, waiting for the film crew, making my drink stretch as long as possible. I was an ordinary citizen enjoying a beer. It was only when I stood up to leave that I heard the sniggers. The barmaid looked at my shrunken trousers and tried to suppress a laugh. I wondered which was better, to be a loathsome tramp or a village idiot, a figure of fun.

Fear; the fear of the unknown. It was with me once more as I prepared to make my bed with the other dossers under the Arches. How vulnerable would I be out in the open? I had no way of telling. Would I be attacked and robbed? I looked anxiously for policemen, not, as before, because I was afraid of arrest, but this time because I felt I needed protection. I had no idea whether the society I was trying to join would accept me, or whether it was a kind of club, a coterie with rules which I might never guess. I was about to find out.

I waited in the doorway of an old theatre some fifty yards away, my dirty woollen hat pulled down against the cold. I had discarded my suitcase in favour of two plastic supermarket bags, one filled with spare clothes, a toothbrush and other odds and ends, the other with newspapers to act as insulation against the cold. I was now wearing my dark blue overcoat, the collar turned up against the damp wind that swept under the railway bridge at Charing Cross. There were about thirty men lying at right-angles to a brick wall under the bridge. Above them I could see a train, its lights on, ready for the off. I could see the passengers settling themselves down, lifting suitcases and bags on to the racks. Many of the men lying on the pavement had climbed inside huge cardboard boxes as a protection against the cold. It was raining steadily, and the wind carried occasional mists of spray across the sleeping bodies. I had been watching for only a few minutes when a portly Irish businessman in a smart blue suit walked by. He stopped and looked me full in the face. For a second, I thought he was going to hit me.

'Would you like a drink?' he asked, nervously.

'I'm sorry?'

'Look,' he said, becoming rather agitated, 'would you like a drink or wouldn't you?'

I looked confused, an expression which seemed to anger him further.

'If you want a drink,' he said, 'I'll buy you one. You can come with me now. So do you want one?'

'No, I don't,' I said.

'Right-ho,' he said, and he walked briskly away.

I was astonished. The whole exchange had lasted only a few seconds. I had little doubt that the nature of his assignation was sexual, yet why had he approached me of all people? If he was a homosexual looking for a pick-up, why had he not gone to one of the more recognized meeting places? And what could he possibly have found attractive about a dosser as dishevelled and forlorn as me? I thought for a minute. Perhaps his motive had been darker, possibly homicidal. After all, what better victim for a sadistic murderer than a tramp whom no one would miss?

It was an experience that disturbed me more deeply the more I thought about it. The world had suddenly become the dangerous place I had feared, a place where sinister men lurked, waiting for the right opportunity to strike. It was how, I thought, many women must feel on the streets of London late at night.

I moved from my shelter in the doorway, and made my way towards the row of cardboard boxes and sleeping bodies. There were only a few vacant spaces, and I was forced to choose a spot near the end of the row, the end nearest the rain. To my left was a man swathed in blankets, half-hidden by what looked like a flat-bottomed boat made of cardboard. To my right there was a more freestyle package, the feet self-contained in a small cardboard box, the body roofed and floored by large sheets of cardboard. Beyond him, an undulating snake of flesh and cardboard stretched as far as the Underground station on the far side of the bridge.

I laid out my newspapers, copies of the *Observer*, the *Sunday Times*, the *Guardian* and the *Daily Mail*. On the pavement, they all looked transparently up-market, and I lay on top of them as quickly as I could, before anyone had a chance to notice. I wondered how long it would be before the cold seeped through. I was wearing all the clothes I had set out with, including those in the suitcase. There was a vest, shirt, two pullovers, a car-coat and my thick overcoat. I wore two pairs of trousers, the inner pair tucked into my socks.

The train which had been standing on the bridge set off. The noise was like a jet aircraft taking off a few yards away, the sound of metal on metal booming and echoing off the iron girders above. None of the sleepers seemed to notice; the man next to me adjusted his cardboard blanket to cover a part of his back which had been left out in the cold. There was not enough cardboard to cover him fully, and he was forced to make constant readjustments throughout the night. I made out a woman sitting further up the line, a round face under a pale knitted bonnet. She did not lie down like the rest at any time in the night, preferring to walk around or snooze on an upturned milk-crate. Next to her was a young black man, deep in thought, like a mathematician solving a vital equation in his head. He stood up and walked to the other side of the street where a specialist collectors' shop still had its bright yellow sign lit. His movements were slow and dignified, like someone in a procession. He reminded me of the sidesmen at my childhood church in Doncaster. I watched him for several minutes as he paced to and fro. Then he stood still and listened. I looked up. There were only pigeons roosting in the girders. A train had moved off a few minutes earlier, but now all was quiet. He slowly turned, and walked in my direction. I observed his face, tranquil and thoughtful, the face of a priest.

'What happened, have you got thrown out of your flat?' He was talking to me, slow deliberate speech, with a strong Yorkshire accent.

'Yeah,' I said, 'my mate chucked me out.'

'Don't worry,' he said. 'Jesus loves you, he'll take care of you. I know. I think God's told me to live with the tramps and preach the gospel of Jesus.' He paused, then he said: 'You look astounded.'

'I am,' I said. 'Does anybody listen?'

'Oh, well, you know, you sow the word, it's like sowing seed, only God can make it grow. You've just got to show a lot of love and listen to people. You know, you've just got to pray, read your Bible. I've got me Bible on me. I read it to that lady there, took me Bible out and read her the twenty-third psalm.'

'And what did she say?'

'She said thank you very much.'

He was twenty-nine years old, born in Jamaica and brought up in Halifax, West Yorkshire.

'I believe Jesus is right here,' he told me. 'I believe the angels are all around here. He might be talking to the angels.' He quoted me the twenty-third psalm, a sonorous recitation which sounded somehow comic, like a child in class who could not read very well.

'The Lord is my shepherd,
I shall not want.
He maketh me to lie down in green pastures,
He restoreth my soul . . .'

His eyes were staring, dark, gentle eyes which never left my face. It was as though he sought my approval. Marks out of ten.

'Thou preparest a table before me,
In the presence of mine enemies.
Thou anointest my head with oil,
And my cup runneth over.
Surely goodness and mercy shall follow me
All the days of my life.
And I shall dwell in the house of the Lord forever.'

He paused, then he said: 'Jesus is the way, man. I used to live my own way, but now I've given my life to Jesus. You haven't to worry about what you eat and what you wear. God'll provide all that. We do worry, sometimes, but God comforts us when we start frettin'. You missed the cup of tea and sandwich at nine o'clock.'

He told me he had once lived in houses and flats, and he had thought he had no friends. But now he felt he had many friends.

'I endured,' he said, 'I kept going. Jesus has made the first move, he's knocking at your heart, it's up to you to make the next move and let him into your heart.'

He seemed tired, and he moved slowly away, resuming his place next to the old woman.

The soup van arrived at around midnight. I had been on the street for nearly three hours and I needed something warm inside. The van was welcome for another reason: it gave me a way of spacing the time, of eking out the night. I suspected that I would not be able to sleep at all, especially if I was to prevent my radio from being stolen. I had already noticed several of my fellow dossers casting envious eyes over it.

As I approached the soup van, two of my fellow dossers began to fight on the pavement, rolling over and over on the cold ground. One seemed to be a man in his seventies, a frail grey-haired skeleton with a hatchet-face. Neither man seemed to have the energy or the co-ordination to do the other serious harm. The other dossers and the charity workers at the soup van ignored them.

The soup itself was thick and delicious, a leek and potato potage with carrots and lentils thrown in for good measure. I could not help thinking that it was as good as some I had enjoyed in expensive London restaurants. A man handed me some bread from a polythene bag. It, too, was delicious, rich wholewheat bread which I dipped into my cup. I thought I detected a vaguely medicinal smell about the bread, as if it had been doctored with some sort of vaccine. I continued to eat; it seemed of little importance.

The trains stopped altogether shortly after midnight, a welcome relief after the thunderous noise of the previous few hours. It seemed very cold, and I doubted that I would be able to sleep at all. I met an old soldier who told me he used to be a regimental sergeant-major. He was six feet six inches tall, he said, but these days he could rarely stretch himself up to his full height. His legs, he told me, were now nearly useless.

'See these crutches?' he said. 'That's what I have to get around on now.'

'How did you get into this state?' I asked him.

'I'm a chronic alcoholic,' he said, almost proudly. 'See these scars?' He showed me wounds on his face which had yet to heal. 'They rob me,' he said. 'They're fine when I'm buying them a drink, but as soon as I've gone over the top, they rob me and they beat me.'

He said he had been a commando in Burma, and he had learnt how to be a violent man.

'Och, I'm a terrible dangerous man, even now,' he said, 'even with these legs. You see that policeman over there, I had the uniform off his back last week. They fined me ten pounds. Criminal damage, they said, and foul words. I ripped his uniform right off his back. He thought he could lift me, because I dinna look much when I'm lying down, but I'm a big fella, six foot six and sixteen stone.'

I looked at his wasted body, and though the frame was big, I doubted he weighed as much as he thought. Perhaps he was thinking back to his days in the army.

A man with a beard who was lying three cardboard boxes further along began to taunt the sergeant-major. He swore back in Gaelic.

'He canna understand what I'm saying,' he told me with a wink. 'Perhaps it's just as well, eh?'

An old woman approached us, carrying a bag of chips from the shop across the street. I thought she was one of the charity workers, but the sergeant-major seemed to know her.

'Sit doon, Annie,' he said. She was dressed in a well-fitting green coat, and wore a neat knitted hat. Her legs were painfully thin, and I guessed she might be twenty years younger than she looked. She offered me a chip.

'You'd better fucking take it,' said the sergeant-major, 'or she'll rear up on you. She will.' I took a chip from her bag.

'I'd give you my last penny,' she told me, glaring into my eyes through thick spectacles. Then she said to the sergeant-major: 'I've got you a sleeping bag, one with a pillow thing in the hood.'

'See what friends I've got,' said the Highlander, 'such good friends,' and he clapped me on the shoulder, a gesture so forceful that he sent me toppling, and I had to reach out to prevent myself falling over altogether.

I slept little that night. At 3.30 the police came to warn us that the street cleaners would soon be arriving and we would have to move. A quarter of an hour later, a massive dustbin lorry pulled round the corner, its hazard lights flashing. Within twenty minutes, they had cleared the litter and all the dossers away. Our night under the Arches was at an end. Only the old hands had managed enough sleep. They had been there since six the previous evening, and they had made sure their cardboard boxes were well lined. I had dozed for barely two hours, and now I was cast adrift to find a warm bolt-hole, somewhere to while away the hours between four in the morning and dawn. I could think of nowhere save the railway stations that would still be open. I drifted towards Waterloo.

I never thought I would be grateful for Muzak. It was the sound of a piano, a great warm generous sound filling the air, flooding every corner of the huge station as I mounted the staircase. I had expected to find Waterloo Station cold and uninviting. Instead, it was a spontaneous concert hall with huge chords from a grand piano echoing round the steel and glass roof like the laughter of a mad artist. I half-expected to find the pianist himself sitting at his piano on one of the platforms, a large brightly coloured scarf around his neck, fingerless gloves on his hands. At the top of the steps the station was empty and a man in a British Rail uniform was sweeping up ready for the week-end trippers. The sound of the piano continued, blurting out from massive speakers around the station concourse. Someone had switched the bland commercial tape for real music. It did not matter, no one was around to hear. I wallowed in the sound. Tired as I was, it made me feel alive, I wanted to shout. Then it stopped abruptly.

'*Pfff, pfff.* This is a staff announcement. Will Driver Collinson, Driver Collinson, please report to the supervisor's office.'

I sat down on a bench seat at the far end of the station, and stared at the ground. The speaker crackled again, and instead of the piano, a cheap vibraphone began to plod its way through a Frank Sinatra standard. Normality was back in all its white-bread glory.

At 6.30, the first trippers began to arrive for the early-morning trains. I sat next to a couple wearing identical university sweatshirts who had propped up their touring cycles against the bookstall. They seemed to be discussing some serious point of politics or economics.

At the far end of the seat a dosser was lying in a sleeping-bag. Two youths passed by, one walking close alongside the bench. As he reached the dosser, he leaned over and shouted in his ear: 'Hey!'

The sleeper's body jerked, and his head appeared from the top of the bag, like a periscope, staring straight at me. He was in his forties, with short grey hair. His eyes were startled, and he reminded me of a wildlife film I had seen of a badger caught in a cameraman's flashlight.

I took out a pen and a scrap of paper, and began to write down my experiences of the night, a diary that was becoming more and more important to me, since it preserved my identity as a person who existed outside the world I had chosen. Sitting there alone, I could hold a conversation with myself which no one else could hear. I sometimes wondered what the other dossers thought of me, scribbling in corners and on park benches;

after all, many of them were illiterate. But my eccentricity had not been challenged or even commented upon.

A group of schoolchildren sat down beside me. The three girls, all aged about sixteen, giggled at me. I was a great joke. The crowds were beginning to thicken now, and the number of dossers, too, began to increase. An old man in a multi-coloured hat shuffled past like a clockwork toy. His feet moved only an inch at a time, and he worked them as rapidly as possible to gain the maximum forward momentum. The effect was unfortunately comic, made more so when, from time to time, his feet appeared to lose traction so that he remained stationary, a mechanism in rapid motion, going nowhere. His clothes were as poor as my own, and as he passed by he looked at me as if appealing for help. Brothers in adversity. I could think of nothing I could do to aid him.

The Badger suddenly sat up again, but this time deliberately, precisely. He unzipped his sleeping-bag and climbed out, fully dressed in a charcoal jacket and fawn slacks. He looked surprisingly dapper, with a cravat at his neck and a pair of natty sandals in the shape of shoes. He combed his hair quickly, rolled up his sleeping bag and squeezed it into a plastic supermarket bag. He had a briefcase which seemed to be filled with spare clothing; this he shut with effort, then he picked up both bag and briefcase and marched smartly towards me. He walked as though he had a business appointment to keep, and he passed so close that I thought he was going to speak. Instead, he made straight for a litter bin by the bookstall. He leaned over it with the air of a surgeon examining a patient. Then he placed his briefcase and bag on the floor, and quickly dipped his hand into the bin. It was such a workman-like action that it had no shame attached to it – here was a professional going about a familiar and necessary task. He plucked out a half-eaten fruit pie and an opened can of Pepsi-Cola, then gathered his bags once more and walked purposefully off into the crowd of travellers.

Later that morning I was joined on my bench by two young alcoholics, both on their way down, but not yet out. She was in her early twenties, a puffy-faced girl with lank brown hair; he, a youth of about the same age in cheap-smart clothes and the flush of alcohol already tinting his pock-marked face. They drank cider from a bottle, finishing off a litre in about twenty minutes. I felt they had chosen me, that they wanted to watch my reactions as they drank, hoping to induce feelings of jealousy in me. As they swigged at the bottle they nudged each other each time I looked up. To them, I was an alcoholic, and their pleasure was to cause me discomfort. The youth stood up and swaggered over to the Gents. He looked back towards his girl friend, amused to see her sitting next to such a tattered derelict as me. The girl continued to drink from the bottle, glancing in my direction, taunting me. It was a great joke. Her boy friend returned, and looked in my direction.

'Aren't you going to introduce me to your friend,' he said, laughing.

I heard a man with an upper-class voice shouting near by.

'You don't deserve to walk on the same planet,' he said. 'You're a brainless facking idiot.' He was a tall man with a black umbrella, and he was rooting in a waste-bin. He pulled out a woman's broken umbrella, then turned again to a man in uniform who was sweeping the concourse near by.

'You've got less facking sense than a facking plank of facking wood,' he yelled.

The sweeper ignored him. The outburst was delivered with such venom that I smiled to myself. My cider-drinking companions laughed out loud, inviting me to share their joy at the old man's tantrum. Here was someone lower on the pecking-order than all three of us. I, like them, was expected to feel comforted by someone else's greater misfortune.

I found a café that lunchtime within a few minutes' walk of the station, where I bought spaghetti bolognese and a cup of tea for 73 pence. It was the first real change of diet I had experienced since I set off, and I relished the change from fish and chips and hamburgers. I was timid about going in at first, cafés were untried territory because of the way I was dressed, but the owner did not seem to mind me at all. Like many cafés run by Italians or Spaniards, he had a clientele largely comprising members of his own family. They spoke in a dialect which sounded half-French, half-Spanish. In the corner of the café nearest the kitchens a social worker and her boy friend were discussing left-wing politics. She sprinkled her arguments with choice horror

51

stories from her casebook. My meal was large, and I felt grateful for the anonymity that the café afforded. A small woman like a frail sparrow sat at the table next to mine with her mentally subnormal son. The café owner addressed him through her.

'A cup of tea for the boy?'

'Yeah, ta,' she replied.

'How's he feeling today?'

'Not too bad.'

As I left, the café owner thanked me generously and asked me to come back soon. As I walked towards Westminster, I felt my fortunes were about to turn.

Oh, great joy! Big Ben was striking 2.30, and I was basking in the sunshine in the garden next to the House of Lords. I had found a sunbed, in perfect working order on a rubbish dump, and I had carried it some half a mile to this spot. At last, I thought, I would be able to catch up on the sleep I had missed the night before, and without causing a fuss, without creating any embarrassment. It seemed an object of great beauty, this simple folding bed, adjustable to all conceivable positions – lightweight, attractive blue canvas finish, rust-free aluminium frame. And it was mine, mine by conquest, mine by right, my first new possession since I took to the streets. I carried it in triumph to the far side of the Victoria Tower Gardens and erected it in the shelter of a huge oak tree. The sun was low in the sky, and its rays shone directly in my face as I sat and watched two Frisbee players running through the autumn leaves on the lawn. A smile came to my face and I closed my eyes. Rest, at last! I opened my eyes briefly, and saw a pretty girl coming towards me. She smiled as she passed; I was the very image of the Happy Tramp.

For the first time I realized how much psychological strain I had been under. I had been welcome nowhere, I had been able to sleep nowhere during the day without harassment or the possibility of arrest, and yet here, in a public park, I was safe, unthreatening and unthreatened. I watched the foreign tourists taking photographs of the House of Lords, many of them so laden with cameras they found it difficult to move freely. The pictures they were taking could be bought for a few pence at any postcard stall, and I wondered at the expense they had gone to to produce images of such banality. None of them noticed me as I watched each in turn make his way to the same spot and take the same photograph. Their money had bought them cameras, but it had not helped them to see.

As the sun disappeared behind the buildings along Millbank, I woke, cold and afraid. There were still people walking in the gardens, but now their steps were more hurried, the cold left them little time to linger. I packed up my sunbed and carried it towards Great Peter Street where I knew there to be a Salvation Army hostel. It was the place I planned to stay that night, though it was now only late afternoon. I walked past the hostel; it seemed dwarfed by the tower block of the Department of the Environment across the street. There were large semi-circular windows on the ground floor which looked like the skylights to a basement. I could hear the sound of voices coming from inside. On the upper floors, the windows looked prison-like, small-paned, mean. It seemed to me a Dickensian, fortress-like building, and I was not looking forward to going inside. I set up my sunbed in the porch of a church about fifty yards up the street. A notice said the church had been badly damaged by fire but that services were still held there. The wind was cold, and I placed the bed alongside the leeward wall, wrapping my coat around me as I tried once more to sleep. Across the street I could see an old man sitting on the wall of an old factory building, rocking to and fro as he slipped in and out of consciousness, falling forward as he fell asleep, pulling himself back as he awoke. He was like a weighted toy in a budgerigar's cage. Three teenaged boys passed by the old man, one of them making sure he was asleep.

They began to smash the windows of the factory, first with stones, then by slamming the opened windows back against the wall. All three climbed into the building through one of the windows they had opened, and the sound of breaking furniture and glass echoed down the street. I felt angry that my sleep was being disturbed, and that I was an impotent witness to their destruction. A fourth youth climbed in through the window. The sound of splintering wood spread to the upper floors, punctuated by laughter, a loud braying laughter. The old man on the wall slept on, still rocking to and fro. Twenty minutes passed, and the sounds continued. I decided to take action. I walked to a telephone box outside the Salvation Army, intending to call the police. I stopped, realizing I would have to give the police an identity. If I were to call myself Tony Crabbe, I might be called as a witness under my fictional identity.

'Hello, is that the police,' I said. 'My name is Rogers, and I've just driven down Monck Street, where I saw a group of four youths breaking into an old factory building ... No, I don't know its name, but it's the only three-storey factory in that street ... They're breaking the place up at the moment ...'

The police arrived five minutes later, first a panda car, then several high-powered squad cars and a police van. The sounds of destruction stopped immediately. I watched from a safe distance, until I was sure the police had found the right building. Then I slowly walked away. I was due to rendezvous with the film crew at Victoria Station, and I walked in that direction past a group of students collecting money for Rag Day. There were three girls and a boy, rattling collecting tins. The boy saw me as a source of fun, and rattled the tin under my nose.

'Contribution to Rag Week?' he said.

The girls began to laugh.

'I'll give you my coat, if you want,' I said.

There was a bird in a cage in the courtyard of the Salvation Army hostel in Great Peter Street, a bright yellow canary in a huge wooden box. It flew aimlessly from side to side, two feet this way, two feet that. From time to time, the inmates reached up to the cage on the wall and fed the bird tit-bits. To the bird, they must have seemed free men.

The hostel had a broad double gate painted bright purple, a gate which looked designed to keep people in. It was nine in the evening when I first knocked.

'Yes?' said a man in a brown overall. He opened the gate only a few inches. I could see an archway behind him.

'I was wondering if you had any free beds for tonight?'

'For two nights?' he said.

I did not understand.

'Yeah,' I said, hoping I had given the right answer. He opened the gate wider.

'Go through there and sit on the chairs. They'll open the booking office shortly.'

The high courtyard was criss-crossed by dark metal fire escapes. There were plants in window boxes down below.

'Through there,' he said, pointing through the archway to the right.

I walked into a bare corridor with gloss-painted walls. An old man was sitting in a row of cheap plastic chairs, holding his head in his hands like a man at prayer. I sat down beside him, and asked how long he had been waiting. He looked up with a start, and seemed hesitant to reply, as if I had asked a trick question.

'About two hours,' he said at length.

His face was ravaged, wrinkled like hands that had been left in hot water too long, and his speech was badly slurred, though he did not seem drunk. He resumed his praying position. Ahead of me I saw a notice-board next to a ticket office window. It read: 'Daily rate £2.20, Weekly rate £13.50 (save £1.90), Full board, £19.50.' I asked the old man where he had slept the previous night. He looked terrified as if I had asked him to confess.

'Why?' he said. His hands were trembling.

'I just wondered,' I said. 'I slept rough last night, and I was wondering if you knew any good places, you know, if I have to do it again.'

He looked relieved.

'Try under Charing Cross,' he said. 'That's the best place.'

'That's where I was,' I said. 'It were a bit cold, though. I had some old newspapers to lie on.'

'Cardboard's best,' said the old man. 'You need cardboard . . . get an old cardboard box.'

He had a bad stutter, and he coughed as he spoke.

'Is there anywhere else where you can sleep rough?' I asked him.

'You can go skippering, sleeping in derelict houses. There are a lot of them round King's Cross, Waterloo, everywhere.'

'How do I find them?'

'You just look for anywhere that's boarded up.'

'And would I need a cardboard box?'

'Y – y – you'd have to. Cardboard is . . . kipper . . . cardboard is thicker.'

He seemed exhausted by this conversation, and rested his head on his knees once more. I could hear the sound of a woman's screams coming from the large room further down the corridor – a television thriller was in progress.

The box office opened at 9.30 and we formed a queue, the old man first, then me. The man behind the glass was small and stocky with a reddish-brown beard and short hair, like a Victorian explorer. He dealt firmly with the old man, asking him to speak up. It was the manner of someone used to receiving abuse from the other side of the glass. The old man said he had stayed before, and he handed over a rumpled five-pound note. It was my turn.

'Can I have just one night?' I said.

'You've been here before, I don't book one night tonight, sir, two only.'

'What happens if I want to move on tomorrow?'

'Well, I'm afraid you'll have to find somewhere else. It leaves us with an empty bed tomorrow. Someone may need it.'

'OK,' I said. It must be some administrative problem which I did not understand, I thought.

'Have you been here before?'

'No, I haven't.'

'I must fill out a place card on you, OK? What's your name?'

He asked me my date of birth and my next of kin, and the place where my mother lived, Doncaster.

'Is that still in Yorkshire?' he asked with a smile. 'You know, when they moved everybody around the . . . you don't know where you end up. Will you sign at the bottom, please?'

It had been a hint of humour, and I was grateful even for that. My bed number was 274. He told me to go to the main room and wait to be called for bed.

I walked down the corridor towards an open doorway. Several men were sitting on chairs by the foot of the stairs, apparently waiting.

The main room was vast, more than a hundred yards long, and

painted uniform cream. There were hundreds of metal lockers running down both walls like the left-luggage department of a station. In between, among the massive iron pillars, were two rows of plastic-topped tables. About 150 men were watching a television set perched high in the far corner, most of them dressed in the poorest of clothes. I was reminded of photographs from the Depression years.

It was just before ten o'clock when the queue for the bedtime cuppa started, a line of men shambling towards the kitchen hatch, some staring blankly, others glancing nervously to one side. Living and partly living. Their clothes were nearly all as threadbare as my own, some gleaming with the patina of continual wear. Only a few wore clothes which were torn – respectability had to be maintained at all costs. I wondered what they thought of me, sitting at an empty table, my overcoat lining showing through two massive rips, the fabric pitted with burns. Did they even wonder how I had reached such apparent despair? No one seemed to consider me too closely; it took enough energy to survive without concerning yourself with other people's misfortunes.

I joined the queue, feeling as if I were stepping into a tableau of nineteenth-century life. It took ten minutes to reach the head of the line. The brown-coated porter asked me what I wanted.

'A cup of tea, please,' I said.

'Ninepence, please, sir,' he said.

I felt extravagantly grateful for the respect he had paid me. I was still smiling as I returned to my table. The tea was sweet, there had been no chance to refuse sugar, and I assumed it had been added to the urn itself. I sat alone; most of the others had crowded at the far end of the room near the television. The screen looked tiny from where I was sitting as the thriller reached one of its many climaxes. The plot was crude, a glossy tale of glamorous girls lured into a life of vice, only to find themselves victims of a sadistic murderer. The sound of their screams echoed eerily round the glossy walls, seeming to increase in volume the further they travelled. Two tables away, I saw a sunken-eyed youth wearing a smart new anorak. There was something desperate about his face, an expression which tried to say 'I'm in control', yet only succeeded in saying 'Help!' He was recounting how he had been released from prison.

'They said I was drunk,' he said, 'but it was a lie. I mean, it was fucking ten o'clock in the morning. How could anyone be drunk at ten in the morning? I was just dizzy. I told them I was dizzy, but they wouldn't believe me.'

The film ended, and the ten o'clock news began. Many of the men turned away from the television and began to talk among themselves. The newsreader talked of an earthquake in Algeria, and of a possible change in the leadership of the British Labour Party. No one seemed to be listening. I saw men reading tabloid newspapers and magazines; one began to sketch something from his imagination on a clean sheet of paper.

At 10.30, almost to the second, a porter appeared at the doorway to the main hall and shouted: 'Going up!'

About twenty men near the television stood like robots and began to walk across the room. I was not sure whether this was the last call for bed, and I decided to join them to make sure I was not left downstairs. Many more men were now standing and moving towards the staircase. The queue tailed back into the main hall, and I saw men taking out their bed tickets and examining the dates printed on them. The queue passed a checkpoint on the first landing.

'Where's your ticket?' said a porter with a clipboard. I handed him my bed ticket, which he tore in two, down a perforated line. 'That's for your breakfast in the morning,' he said, and he handed back the other half. He entered my number on a register, and while he was writing I noticed a door which looked as though it would completely seal off the staircase on this bottom landing.

'Do you lock the door?' I asked.

'In a minute,' said the porter.

I made my way up to the third landing. My room was C1 on the second floor. On the stairs were groups of men having a last cigarette before turning in for the night. I inspected the lavatory on the landing immediately below my room. There was soft toilet tissue – a luxury I had not expected. I listened to the men's conversation outside. From the landing below I heard an Irishman holding forth to two friends.

'Shakespeare,' he said, 'I wouldn't give you tuppence for him.

There's not a person can even understand what he's getting at.'

The others argued passionately in Shakespeare's favour, claiming no other country could match him for style and range.

'There's one thing you can say for him,' said one. 'He wasn't fucking Irish.'

I washed in a large white basin, drying my face on toilet paper. On the landing outside my room two men were apparently showing each other their new clothes.

'And it's got three inside pockets,' said one, demonstrating first the left, then the right-hand lining of his jacket. 'I've never had three inside pockets before.'

The other man studied the lining of his own jacket.

'I've only got the one,' he said.

The entrance to the dormitory was a large iron double door. It had a black rubber buffer to stop the doors clanging to. Inside, it was very dark; I could make out the shape of the windows I had seen from the outside. In the gloom, they looked even more prison-like than before. I could see long rows of beds, dozens of them in four lines. They seemed to stretch nearly a hundred yards to my left along the vast bare room. I leaned forward to read the numbers painted on the frames: '262', '263'.

My bed must be on the far side of the room, I thought. I squeezed past two rows of beds, and began to look for the numbers again: '272, 273, 274,' I read. I had arrived. It seemed like a hospital bed, except the metal frame was painted black. The sheets looked clean, and I turned them back to see if there had been a previous occupant. They felt crisp and freshly ironed. The bed was facing the windows overlooking the street, and I could make out the plate glass of the Department of the Environment building opposite. I had visited those offices several times as a reporter, interviewing Ministers of the Crown, talking with smooth public-relations men in carpeted offices. The building towered above me, and I could not help but feel the heavy symbolism of my present lowly position.

I heard the heavy snoring of men asleep; seventy-five beds, about three quarters of them occupied. There were about eighteen inches between each bed, close enough almost to feel the breath of your neighbour as he slept. I undressed slowly, making sure my clothes covered my radio and my plastic bag. I

59

took off my filthy vest with some relief, though it looked far worse than it was. I made the pile of clothes under the bed as precarious as possible so that a thief would find it difficult to steal anything without making a noise. It felt luxurious to slide between the cool, clean sheets, a pleasure so intense I gasped with enjoyment. All around me was the sound of old men coughing and young men farting. The fart seemed to be as much a humorous device as a physical need, a pithy statement delivered to an audience, like a one-line joke. Mostly duration and volume were the criteria for success, but there were endless variations on the central theme. A man a few beds to my right attempted a kind of wolf-whistle, a distinct rising and falling cadence with a brief pause between phrases. He was answered almost immediately by a short rasping fart from the row of beds behind me, an insult intended purely for its shock value. I guessed that some of the men must have deliberately stored wind for the nocturnal ensemble. By the time I fell asleep, I had endured as many as twenty variations on a theme.

It was about one in the morning when I heard a repetitive slapping sound, like a wet sheet in the wind. A voice said: 'You fucking black bastard.'

I sat up, and saw a long-haired white youth standing over the bed facing me. He was hitting someone, his arms rising like the sails on a windmill and crashing down on the man's face and body.

'I'll sue you,' said the victim. His accent sounded African, Nigerian perhaps. The white youth launched another attack, his arms flailing wildly.

'Shut your fucking mooth, ya black bastard,' he shouted. The black man tried to shield his face with his hands.

'I've told you . . . I'll sue you,' he said. 'You're not going to get away with this, my friend . . . this will lead to court action.' His voice rose above the sound of the blows.

'Shut up, you fucking black cunt,' said the Scotsman, continuing his attack.

The door behind me opened violently, and a porter rushed in with a torch. He shone it directly at the Scot.

'What's going on?'

'I was just sorting something out with this bastard,' said the Glaswegian, panting. He had a pleasant, open face, a look almost of innocence.

'Well, get back to your bed, you can sort anything out in the morning,' said the porter. 'There are people trying to get some sleep.'

The Scot stood his ground. He looked dazed, half-blinded by the light from the torch.

'Back to your bed,' said the porter.

'I have nae finished wi' him yet,' said the Scot. Even now his face looked honest, appealing.

'Get back to your bed, or you're out,' said the porter. The Scot moved slowly towards the far end of the room. He was fully dressed. The torch followed him to his bed, where he took off his jacket and started to undress. The porter walked towards the door.

'Good night, lads,' he said, and he left.

From the darkness, the Scot shouted: 'I'll still get you, you black bastard.'

The African shouted back: 'I'll sue you for every penny you've got.'

'Well, you won't get very fucking much, then, will you?'

'Oh, shut up,' said another voice from my end of the room.

'You fucking shut up,' said the Nigerian.

'Shut up yourself, you black bastard.'

'I'll sue you, too,' said the Nigerian.

There was silence for a few minutes. I closed my eyes once more. Suddenly from about seven beds further up the room I heard the sound of fighting again. In the half-light I could make out the same Scot attacking another man, a man who seemed to have a Mohican hair-cut. The Scot was joined by a second man, who held the victim while the Scot kicked and punched him. The moans of the injured man grew louder.

I heard him say: 'Give up, will you? Fucking stop it.'

He seemed to be in no position to defend himself. The blows increased in intensity, some twenty or thirty kicks and punches to the face and body. The Glaswegian seemed to be out of control, like a hydrophobic dog, cursing and swearing. He began

61

to raise his foot even higher, trying to kick his victim full in the face as he sat in his bed. It was an effort which almost caused him to overbalance.

'Fucking stop it!' said the man in the bed, his hands clasped round the back of his head.

'Shut up, you bastard, I'm a member of staff,' said the Scot.

A voice from the far end of the room shouted: 'Fucking well stop all that fighting.'

The Glaswegian stopped for a moment, then he screamed: 'I'm a member of staff, so shut your fucking mooth, or you'll be next.'

He continued to hit the Mohican, though now he seemed to be tiring. The door burst open once more, and two brown-coated porters rushed in, holding torches. The fighting stopped immediately. The room lights, a row of closely shaded bulbs down the centre of the room, were switched on, revealing the two men standing over the Mohican's bed, their fists still clenched. They were both breathing heavily.

'Right, you two . . . out,' said the burliest porter, a man of about six foot two whose close-cropped hair gave him a pugnacious air. 'Come on,' he repeated.

The two men began to gather their belongings, and walked out of the room without further protest. Their manner suggested not so much contrition as satisfaction.

Just then, a half-caste man at the farthest corner stood up, shaking with rage.

'Bloody staff brutality, you bastards,' he said. 'I'll take you to court.'

'What's that?' said the burly porter with a look of exaggerated astonishment. 'Are you accusing the staff of brutality . . . are you?'

'There's no use denying,' said the man; his accent was West Indian. 'We all saw it.'

'Listen,' said the porter, 'we're the only members of staff in this room. Are you accusing us?'

'Yes, and I'll take you to court tonight.'

The porter spun round in exasperation. He could hardly believe it.

'I'm not staying here a minute longer,' said the West Indian.

'It's not safe with you bastards hitting we all night long. I'll take you to court over this, you see.'

'Fucking shut him up, will you, and let us get some sleep,' said a man in a bed close to the West Indian.

'You'll see if I'm not right,' said the West Indian. 'Brutality, and it's not the first time. This place is a madhouse. I ain't staying, I tell you.'

He began to pack his bags, pausing occasionally to continue his outburst, then packing again. His shouting went on for another ten minutes, then he left. The porter switched out the lights, and stood by the doorway, his torch shining in the darkness. He addressed the room as a whole.

'Sorry about the disturbance, gentlemen, good night.'

His torch flashed, and he was gone. Tired as I was, I found it hard to get to sleep. Every new sound made me open my eyes with a start.

The following day, I asked the Mohican why he had been attacked.

'I don't know,' he told me. 'I didn't even know them blokes, apart from seeing them down here in the main room.'

I began to realize how lucky I had been the previous night. It might just as easily have been me who was selected as a target, instead of the Mohican or the black man.

At breakfast, the fight was the main topic of conversation.

'They're fucking head-bangers, those Scotch bastards,' said a man who looked like a Greek. 'I'll tell you something, I was on the landing having a quiet smoke, just standing there in my bare feet, and this first Scotch bastard comes out and asks me what size boots I took. "Size nine," I tell him. Then he throws this lighted cigarette on the floor, and he says "Good, I've been looking for a size-nine foot to stamp that bugger out." '

I thought the story sounded like a stand-up comedian's joke, but the Greek was perfectly serious.

'Anyway,' the Greek continued, 'he looked as though he'd fucking murder me if I didn't tread on the fucking thing, so I trod on it. The bastard. Then this second Scotch bastard comes out and asks me the same question. So I thought, if I say I take a small size in boots, perhaps he won't fucking bother. I told him size seven and he says: "Great, I've been looking for a size-seven foot to put that bastard out," and he throws down another cigarette on the floor.'

I tried hard to suppress a smile. The whole story sounded ludicrous. I could not be sure if the Greek was serious.

A red-haired bricklayer from Leicester said: 'It's bloody bad enough having to live in this place, without having to put up with all that. I wasn't in your room, but we all heard the screaming and shouting.'

I asked him what he was doing in London. He said he was looking for work.

'I'm trying to get work as a brickie eventually,' he said, 'but all my tools are still in Leicester. I'll get the wife to bring them down later on. I've been looking for any sort of job in the meantime. You know, labouring, casuals, anything.'

He showed me a list of jobs he was thinking of applying for. It included casual work at the BBC, my own employers. He gave me an address in Croydon where he said a firm was wanting painters and decorators.

'It's a bit far out for me,' he said. 'I mean, if you want somewhere cheap to live you've got to come to a place like this in the centre. Then you can't afford all the travelling. The trouble is, there aren't many jobs for ordinary blokes in the centre, it's all office stuff. When I get me tools down, I should be able to make enough to move somewhere else.'

I joined the queue for a second cup of tea. There were four Glaswegians immediately behind me. One of them, a burly man with a moustache, was wearing a bright blue track-suit, the top not quite matching the bottom. An old man sitting at a table near by was talking loudly.

'I can't do it,' he told a porter who was clearing the tables. 'I've got this thing in the middle of my foot.'

'Yes,' said the porter, 'so have I, it's called a toe.'

'Well, you must be bloody deformed if you've got a toe in the middle of your foot,' said the old man, and he laughed.

'I've got trouble with this thing in the middle of my legs,' said the burly Glaswegian.

'Well, the Salvation Army can't help you there,' said the old man. 'Corns, yes; bunions, yes; but cocks, never.'

*

It was a few minutes before nine in the morning, and I stood in the courtyard near the huge gates. The walls were whitewashed up to the first-storey level, and the climbing plants in the window boxes struggled towards the light. The canary flitted in the shadow of the massive gabled roof of its cage on the far wall, a blur of yellow against the black. I looked up at the dormitory windows above. They had a kind of beauty, the massive beauty of the prison yard.

As I left through the main gate, the porter said: 'If you go out now, you won't be allowed back until 11.30.'

I thanked him and stepped into the street. To my surprise, it was a bright and sunny morning. I walked quickly up the street and round the corner, feeling a great sense of release. It was Sunday morning, and Westminster Abbey was already in business. The opulence of the building and the well-dressed people in the yard near by overwhelmed me by their contrast with the poverty of the world I had just left. I could not tell which world seemed less real.

As I passed through Parliament Square I noticed the black man who had recited the twenty-third psalm to me under the Charing Cross Arches. He was standing with an old man in ragged clothes and speaking slowly, deliberately. The old man seemed to be only half-listening. When, I wondered, did the preacher sleep? I sat in a doorway opposite the House of Commons and waited for the film crew. I felt more tired than the previous morning and I could not immediately explain why. Even with the traumas of the violence in my dormitory, my bed had been comfortable and I had been asleep for as much as eight hours. Perhaps only now was my body beginning to register the shock of my night on that cold pavement.

A smart man in a grey suit strode out towards St James's Park and Buckingham Palace. He carried a rolled umbrella, and he seemed to have an appointment to keep. He, like me, was one of the residents of the Great Peter Street Salvation Army hostel. I saw him again that night, queueing for his evening meal, his rolled umbrella hanging from his arm. He took his tray to a table in the centre of the room where three other men were sitting. None of them seemed to know him. He hung the umbrella on the edge of the table and addressed himself to his meal. He sat upright, correct, holding his knife and fork precisely, concentrating on the food, apparently oblivious of everything around him. I sat behind him, eating my three slices of black pudding, two slices of bread and butter, and drinking a cup of sweet tea. I felt my ragged appearance must be giving him displeasure, but he did not seem to notice me. He might have been in a first-class restaurant on the French Riviera. He finished his meal and went over to a locker near the door. Inside were clean towels, toiletries, clothes; everything was neatly arranged. He took out a book and sat down at a near-by table to read. He spoke to no one.

I met a gentle-faced man with hair like that of an Afghan hound, a hippie left over from the 1960s, his mind burned out by drugs. He was drawing a picture of a spaceship which had a clown's face.

'There's another one there,' he said, his finger on the picture. 'That's a patrol ship. It's a magic universe.'

His friend was short-haired and mad-eyed, like a man pleading for his life. He told me he was a musician who played the flute, saxophone and guitar. But he had never been able to afford an instrument of his own, he said, and he did not like the way that such possessions would tie him down. He played me a soft and haunting blues on a harmonica which was barely audible over the crashing echoes from the television. He had real talent.

'Have you ever dropped LSD?' said the artist.

'No,' I said.

He began to nod, a wise nod of agreement with himself. The musician pointed at the picture and began to give his friend advice.

'Why don't you make the bottom of it into a giant planet?' he told his friend. 'You could build a huge Smarties factory in the bottom right-hand corner, then you could sell it as an advert to the Smarties people.'

The artist smiled at me with his slow, tired eyes. He began to follow his friend's command like a machine whose batteries were almost exhausted, stopping short only as his pen was about to touch the paper. Then he woke up, and looked at me as if we had shared some big private joke.

*

That night I felt I was sleeping in the geriatric ward of a hospital. The man in the next bed coughed all night, a desperate, bottomless cough which left him gasping for air. I found myself wanting to clear my own throat. It was one in the morning by the time I fell asleep. At five, I became aware of a porter shining his torch into the face of the man in the next bed.

'Five o'clock, five o'clock,' he said.

By 7.30, half the beds in the dormitory were empty. By eight o'clock only one man was still asleep.

'Come on, sir, time to get up,' said the porter. 'Wake up, sir. The major will be round in a minute, and he won't like it. He's still angry about that do on Saturday night, so we don't want him to find you still in bed. Come on, wake up.'

'I have woken up,' said the man, lifting his head from his pillow.

'Yes, but I want to see you get up.'

'I am up.'

'No, you're not, you're lying down. That's better. Thank you, sir.'

The reluctant riser was a lumpy man with a curly brown beard. He looked at my radio, and began to girate in his underwear.

'Funky music,' he said, with a smile.

'I can only get Radio Two,' I said.

After breakfast I asked the man in the booking office if it was possible to stay another night.

'Have you been to Social Security?' he asked.

'No,' I said.

'Well, if you're going this morning, don't book in for a night. Go to the next window, and they'll give you a letter saying you stopped here last night. Take it to Social Security, and they'll either give you a voucher or some cash for a week. I wouldn't book in for tomorrow night, otherwise you lose that for one night, you see.'

I went to the next window, where a woman handed me an envelope.

'OK, Scarborough Street,' she said.

I stood in the courtyard, anxious to get outside to open the envelope and find out what it said. There was a short queue for the gate, and as I waited I noticed the man with the rolled umbrella bending over a tap in the yard, filling a plastic beaker with water. He leaned forward to drink it, making sure no drops fell on his three-piece suit. He had hung his umbrella on a fire escape while he refilled the beaker for a second cup of water. Then he joined me in the queue. Outside, I walked the same route as the one I had seen him take the previous day, hoping to catch sight of him once more. But he had disappeared round the first corner. I made my way to Buckingham Palace, where I sat down on an ornamental wall and opened the letter from the Salvation Army to the Social Security Office. It read:

> The Salvation Army Men's Hostel
> 18 Great Peter Street,
> Westminster,
> London SW1
> Manager, Major D. Baxter

Department of Health and Social Security

Dear Sirs,

Re. Tony Crabbe 274

The above-named gentleman has been booked in at this hostel for 2 nights. He is due to re-book on 13.10.80.

A *voucher* for Bed/Breakfast and Evening Meal would be appreciated.

Thanking you,

Yours sincerely,
David Baxter (Major).

I folded the note, and looked towards Buckingham Palace. Once again, I was a character in my own play.

I felt stiff. My role as a down-and-out called for a great deal of stooping. Those who held themselves too erect, too confidently, were automatically suspect. My waist and my back were beginning to ache, and I started stretching and bending exercises on the pavement. A coach carrying German tourists stopped near by, and I saw dozens of faces turn from the sights they had come to see, to view a ragged man touching his toes. Scarecrows were not supposed to move.

I set off for the East End of London, where I planned to find accommodation at one of the two cheap commercial hotels which I knew catered for dossers. I was becoming used to walking long distances. My route took me through Bloomsbury, where I intended to pass Charles Dickens's old house in Doughty Street. It seemed a natural thing to do, since so much of the world I was discovering appeared little different from the one he described in *Oliver Twist* and *Hard Times*.

The idea of a destination, of a purpose, made me stride out. I became aware of people stepping to one side to let me pass. The same looks of contempt were there, the same feeling of mass moral judgement, but now there was also a sense of alarm. Why should a derelict look so determined, what could a person like him be in such a hurry about? Several people turned and looked at me as I walked by. I passed Coram Fields, where nurses were taking children to play in the park. One of them shepherded her charges out of my path; once inside the park they would be safe from such dangerous men – adults were not allowed there unless accompanied by a child. I had by this time grown immune to the shame of provoking such responses. I could now put myself in their position, since it was futile to demand that other people should recognize me for my inner self.

By the time I reached Guilford Place, I was walking quite fast. I passed within six feet of one of the BBC executives who had helped to plan the whole project I was engaged in. His eyes avoided mine, and he walked on. I noted down the time and place, and the details of his clothing, to prove that the encounter had actually occurred.

I stood outside Charles Dickens's house for several minutes. It was a museum which charged admission for entry, and I decided I could not afford to go inside. I thought about the descriptions of the workhouse in *Oliver Twist*, and I wondered what Dickens would have made of the Welfare State that had replaced it. It was true that the world I had come to know no longer restricted the diet of the poor to the small quantities of

69

water and oatmeal he had described – three meals of thin gruel a day with an onion twice a week and half a roll on Sundays. With the £2 a day I had remaining after I had paid for my hostel accommodation, I was able to buy three good-sized hamburgers a day, and three glasses of milk – a reasonably healthy diet. Yet, to do so, to spend all my money on food would leave me with little hope of escaping from the narrow band of society in which I found myself.

And how narrow my life had become! Even as Dickens had described how the workhouse poor were separated into single-sex accommodation, was I not also confined to the eternal bachelorhood of the poor? My world was desperately masculine, a brutish, segregated existence of solitary pleasure, where heavy drinking seemed a natural response, even though it led to continued imprisonment in the same restricted stratum of mankind.

I walked on through the Inns of Court, past a group of lawyers in a courtyard of the Inner Temple. They were discussing their timetable for the following day.

'I'm sorry,' said one, 'I simply must go to Oxford first thing. I'm afraid that's absolutely definite.' It, too, was a voice from a different age.

The river lapped over the buttresses of Blackfriars Bridge, an angry, dirty, proletarian stream sweeping east towards the sea. I saw an old derelict making his way up the wooden staircase from HMS *President*. He carried three or four plastic bags, and he gave me a guilty stare as he passed. Had he found a place to sleep, I wondered, somewhere in the dry where he had not been disturbed until this late hour of the afternoon? It seemed unlikely. I moved on.

The river seemed swollen, a seething brown that left a damp patch some two feet above the waterline. I watched the traffic passing up and down the murky water. A police launch dawdled along the far bank, a tug-boat ploughed downstream. I climbed down the steps under Blackfriars Bridge and walked along by the water. There was a railway bridge with arches almost low enough for me to touch. Below me I could see the road. Why, I wondered, did no one sleep here at night, instead of under the bridge at Charing Cross? Perhaps the river was too close or the exhaust fumes from the traffic too dense. And down here, I thought, there were no policemen to stop the dossers from being mugged.

At London Bridge I climbed the stairs to the pavement on the east side. It was five o'clock. I had been dawdling. As I emerged, I found myself being swept along in a great tide of people, thousands of office workers half-walking, half-running in a desperate race to the other side. I was reminded of the start of cross-country races at school, the jostling for position, the zig-zagging past your opponents, the savage need to break from the pack. From the tranquillity of the embankment I found myself, without reason, walking as fast as the others, swinging my plastic carrier-bag rapidly to and fro, keeping pace with briefcases and handbags, executive cases and folders, short stubby umbrellas hung from the arm, long thin ones swaggered from the wrist. I was nearly half-way across before it occurred to me to slow down.

It took a great effort of will to stem the tide. As I resumed my desultory pace, I was jostled from behind by fierce businessmen anxious to get ahead. I held my ground, creating a log-jam behind and an eddy of calm in front. Three office workers spun past into the tranquil space, the two men observing the slow swing of the buttocks of the girl in front.

All around them, the rush continued, quickening in pace as we approached the other side, where the trains from London Bridge Station were visible. One of the men in office suits caught his friend by the arm and shouted, 'Come on!' and they dashed towards the station. I was spun off at a tangent as the crowd sped round the corner. I felt like rubbish washed up on a beach. I had arrived at Tooley Street.

It was a scruffy riverside canyon, the dark tradesmen's entrance to the City. Its gallows atmosphere had inspired some showman to open a shrine to murder and torture under the railway bridge, a waxworks designed to frighten small children. I walked past towering warehouses topped by the gibbets of cargo-cranes, on into the gloom of the tall and narrow street and to the Tooley Hotel. It was an unsentimental building, a place that made no concessions to the soft-furnishing side of human nature. I was grateful that this was to be only a preliminary visit, a chance to see if it had any free rooms, and a chance to change my mind about staying there altogether.

In the hallway was a notice telling the residents that the television set would not be replaced, since four previous sets had been smashed by them and the rental company had come to the end of its patience. I asked the concierge how much it would cost to stay among such forthright critics of the very medium I worked for.

'One pound forty-four a night,' he said.

I decided to inspect the rooms later. I was glad to be in the open air again while the afternoon light still held. I walked towards Tower Bridge, where I scented the sweet smell of beer being brewed near by. It seemed a sinfully sweet odour, and I leaned against the railings on Tower Bridge, breathing it in, swallowing huge gobbets of air like a man in a sauna bath. I had spent 27 pence on half a pint of bitter three days before, and I had begun to crave the taste of food and drink that would satisfy more than mere hunger. I had not realized how bland my diet had become.

I crossed to the centre of the bridge, and like all the tourists, I stopped to look down the crack in the middle. I craned my head to view the great stone towers. A few yards away, a German couple had stopped a bearded old man who carried a plastic carrier-bag like my own.

'Excuse me, sir,' said the woman, 'could you kindly tell us how ze bridge verks?'

'It lifts up in the middle,' said the dosser, 'and the two sides sort of fold back up to the towers.'

The woman relayed this information to her husband.

'Und how,' she said to the dosser, 'does ze mechanism operate?'

'I don't really know,' said the old man, after some thought.

The woman turned to me.

'Do you know how ze mechanism operates?'

'What?' I said, astonished that she should be treating dossers as tourist guides. 'Well, I suppose there are counterweights inside the towers.'

The old man looked at me oddly. I had used a word outside a dosser's normal vocabulary. I decided to walk on. As I left, I heard the old dosser say: 'That's right, there's weights in the towers.' He seemed genuinely pleased to help. The German couple nodded, and began to point to the towers.

I had been told that I would not want to stay in the Tower Bridge Hotel, and I checked in that night knowing I would not be staying long. It was a former public house on the wrong side of Tower Bridge, and it now catered for a more serious drinking clientele. The smell of their rancid sweat was evident even from the street, and I pushed open the hardboard door with a feeling of nausea. It was a high-ceilinged entrance room, fronted by huge dirty panes of glass and dominated by a long empty bar, like a saloon in a Wild West ghost town. A drunken man was lounging against a doorway, steadying himself. He seemed to be about to leave.

'Excuse me,' I said. He turned, apparently unsure of where the sound had come from. 'Is this the Tower Bridge Hotel?'

'The office is over there,' he said, waving wildly to the far end of the room. There was a doorway behind the bar, and I could hear the sound of a science-fiction serial on a television set. It was a large room, so badly stained with nicotine that it looked as though it might have been in a fire. This must have been one of the public rooms when it was still a pub, I thought. A half-made bed stood in one corner, fenced off by a water-pipe which ran at knee height the full width of the room. A kitten was asleep on a chair, and in the near corner a shabby man sat behind a desk piled high with paper. He had been watching the television, warming himself on an electric fire, and he struggled to make himself look business-like. On top of the television a toilet roll stood like an ornament.

'It's one seventy per night,' he said, 'ten pound a week.'

'I only want one night,' I said.

'Well, I might have C2B free,' he said, 'might have.' He began to shuffle through the papers on his desk, flicking through a scruffy hotel register. The kitten woke at the sound of the voices and jumped on to the desk. It curled up on the register, but the manager made no attempt to move it, preferring to peer through the gap between its paws at the complex lists of numbers and names.

'C2B might be free,' he said, 'or there might be a bed in whatsisname next door.'

'Is the pipe still in use?'

He looked at the pipe running across the room as if it had just sprung up when he wasn't looking.

'No, I think it's been disconnected,' he said. 'It was for steam. Or it may have been for gas.'

He took my money and felt first in his left pocket and then in his right for change. Then he said we had better go upstairs and ask the other residents which beds were free. He led me through the foyer where three drunks were broaching a few bottles of cider. They watched us pass with interest, handing the bottle one to the other. At the end of the bar we entered a hardboard tunnel which seemed to have been recently installed as a fire precaution. The manager held the door open for as long as possible, apparently unable to find a light switch. I stumbled, barely keeping my feet. Near the top of the stairs the landlord turned and pointed to my radio.

'I'd leave that in the office if I were you,' he said. 'You know, we have some blokes in here who . . . I'm not saying they would, mind, but you know, it could whatsisname . . .'

'I'll use it as a pillow,' I said.

'I don't think you will have any trouble,' he said. 'There's some quite decent blokes, you know . . . but . . .'

We passed through a fire door into another hardboard tunnel. At the end of the darkness we entered a high room with windows overlooking the street. There were twelve beds, most of them double bunks, several of them occupied by sleeping men, even though it was only eight in the evening. The smell of sweat was now mixed with the thick stench of vomit, an odour which made me feel sick. On the far wall I saw spatterings of what looked like half-digested food, and I almost turned to walk out. The manager stalked around the room as if he were looking for a mouse. Periodically, he stopped at the end of a bed and looked at the number painted on the frame. Then he looked around the room at the other beds, as though he were counting. A dark-haired Scotsman was lying in a bed under one of the windows, his blankets drawn up under his chin.

'The top one's empty,' he said, looking towards the bunks in the corner. 'Anderson never come back.'

'Is that C2B?' said the manager.

'Aye.'

'Which one, the top or the lower?'

'The top, an old Irishman got TB was in it.'

'Are you sure? Are you sure about that?' said the manager.

'I don't fancy catching bloody TB,' I said.

'No, no, no,' said the manager, 'lots of chaps, er . . . whatsisname . . . I can't tell, it's like you come in, I wouldn't know if you'd got something like that. I mean a chap doesn't need a bleeding medical or nothing. If it's you or me, yeah, but not unless you direct him.'

The manager's words did little to comfort me, and he seemed to sense that I was about to demand my money back. He led me quickly back along the tunnel into the room next door, where he woke a crippled man in a bottom bunk. The man's artificial limbs were propped up against his pillow, the trousers and shoes still on them.

From the other side of the room, a huge man with a grey tousled mane of hair lurched forward in his upper bunk like a character in a low-budget horror film.

'*Baddadaaaa!*' he yelled. '*Raahtcursssss!*'

'Hold your ruddy noise,' said the manager, approaching the man like a lion tamer, holding his arms out to keep him back. 'He's booked in the same as anybody else . . .'

'*Blonnayouwww!*' shouted the lion.

'Just get your bloody head down, shut your noise,' said the manager.

The wild man uttered a series of grunts, then slumped back on to his bed. Within seconds he was asleep again. The manager went to fetch me a clean sheet for my bed, but I had already decided to leave. The drunks seemed too unpredictable for me to have any chance of sleep, and I did not think I could count on the manager for help if I was in trouble. He brought me the sheet, and left me alone. I stole from room to room like a thief, checking the conditions in the rest of the hotel. A portly naked man with a cigarette in his mouth strolled past me in the corridor.

I was very depressed by the time I made my way back down the stairs into the foyer. The drinking party was in full swing, the men already on their third bottle of cider. An Irishman approached me and asked politely if I had any food to spare. His eyes were out of control, and I was astonished he could still stand.

'Anything at all,' he said. 'I'd go out and look for some fish and chips or somethin', only I'm too fucking drunk to walk. Just give me a sausage roll, or anything you've got.' His speech was almost unintelligible, and he stumbled towards me, grabbing my carrier-bag. He pulled out my old sweater and my A to Z street atlas.

'No, nothin',' he said, satisfied I had been telling the truth. He zig-zagged his way back to his seat, then changed his mind and tried to make it through the door leading to the bedrooms.

'Sorry for having troubled you,' he said, leaning hard against the wall. 'Good night.' And he slithered off into the darkness.

He had been one of the politest drunks I had ever met; but, I wondered, how quick would he have been to lose his temper when the opposite mood took him?

I set off for the Tooley Hotel a couple of hundred yards up the street. I did not hold out much hope that it would be any better; after all, it was 26 pence cheaper than the hotel I had just left.

The receptionist was not a man given to the hard sell.

'Your room is I-one, up to the first floor, and keep turning right,' he said. He might have been issuing tickets to a funeral.

I climbed a flight of concrete steps into a claustrophobic blind maze of hardboard partitions. There was the familiar stench of sweat, and I saw a half-eaten ham sandwich lying on the floor on the landing; above it, a brown smear on the wall where someone had wiped his hand. Behind the partitions, I could hear the sound of bed-springs as men turned over in their sleep. Each partition was open at the top, a design feature which enabled the electric lights in the corridors to light the rooms at no further cost. It took me several minutes to find my room. I tiptoed down several blind legs of the maze before doubling back towards the front of the building. Inside the room were four beds, and a stocky man with a crew-cut lay sleeping beneath the window overlooking the street. My bed seemed to have clean linen. I returned to the landing at the top of the stairs where I found the washroom, a badly neglected affair with broken basins, no soap, and a towel dispenser that had jammed. There were sodden newspapers on the floor, some of them trailing into the gutter of the urinal. The two lavatories were horribly fouled.

These two commercial hotels seemed to cater almost exclusively to the needs of the heavy drinker.

On my way back downstairs, I passed a man almost unconscious through drink, dragging himself up the handrail. Another, an old man with long dirty grey hair, wandered around, apparently unaware of my presence. I decided to stay the night. At least my room seemed tolerable, and the stranger in the bed by the window did not look like the sort of man to do me any harm.

He was rosy-cheeked, plump and broad-shouldered, like a farm-boy. He wore a short, tight sweater which looked several sizes too small; it was his sole night attire. As he made another of his many trips out of the room that night, he reminded me of babies I had seen playing on the beach. At four o'clock that morning I woke to see his half-naked silhouette at the window, gulping water from a soft-drinks bottle.

At 7.30, he dressed quickly and left, carrying no luggage. I followed shortly afterwards, anxious to escape the claustrophobia of those dark narrow corridors and the dark narrow street outside.

My days were spent increasingly in libraries. I became a connoisseur of the warm corner, of the more obscure category of bookshelf where only the overseas students dared to tread. I developed an expertise in sleeping positions which, to the casual observer, looked like devoted study. I would prop my head in my hands and pretend to read a tome on a particularly fine point of tort or electronics. I would rest an arm on the desk, then lower my head in a simulation of extreme myopia, and pretend to write. Whenever I woke, I found it hard to distinguish between my cozenage and the real thing, as perpetrated by my fellow academicians.

I found it unjust that the staff often took it upon themselves to sort out the bored sheep from the dissembling goats when both categories seemed to me guilty of a sublime waste of time.

'Try not to go to sleep,' said the man in St Pancras Library, prodding me into life. The way he said it, it sounded like, 'Try not to murder your wife.'

In the dining hall of Bruce House, a spike-haired punk was doubled up on a dining chair, his head on his knees, like a puppet whose strings had been cut. All the tables and chairs from the evening meal had been cleared away around him, leaving him stranded like a bottle on a mud bank. A cleaner swept rubbish into a pile near by.

A notice on the dining-room wall said: 'No more than five hundred people in this dining hall at any one time.'

It was a vast local-authority hostel where for £1.65 you could buy squalor, danger and neglect; a place where you prayed there would never be a fire.

The tiles were pleasant, of course. They had been commended by experts for the beauty of their scenes of Dutch rural life, ceramic idylls of peasants at work, girls in clogs, windmills in full sail. And even if the sheer quantity of tiles made the hostel look a little like a residential subway, they were still the good side of Bruce House.

I was amazed by the scale of the place from the start: the huge public rooms where men herded like sheep around television sets or sat in corners passing the bottle. In my later visits I was shocked by the violence, too, by the drunks who rampaged unchecked, picking fights with anyone who caught their eye. I was shocked by the scale of the squalor, of the litter piled everywhere, the chairs left upturned, the fouled bedding lying in the corridors. But most of all I was shocked by the callousness of the fire precautions which put the security of the building above the safety of the inmates by the simple expedient of locking the means of escape.

I arrived in mid-evening, booking in through the heavy turnstiles that marked the barrier between the inside and the outside world. Like much else I was to discover about Bruce House, they were symbols of a system of control which existed only in theory. As I waited for my change, I watched men come and go through the turnstiles unchecked – the barriers might as well not have existed, I thought.

I had been issued with a cubicle number – 386 – and I asked a rosy-faced Welshman to explain the system.

'There's a whistle every half-hour,' he said. 'When you hear it, you go and queue up on the stairs until they open the gates.'

I looked around first. There was a dining hall like a huge corridor around a central well, where men were playing games of poker. The canteen had closed, and only a man brewing his own tea in a corner was left. I saw several discarded stoves in one corner – evidence of a two-million-pound renovation scheme that the building was undergoing after a recent public outcry.

I smelt the acid scent of urine before I entered the main lavatories. The floor was awash; there were old newspapers lying everywhere, most of them soaked through; none of the thirty or so WC cubicles had any toilet paper. In the dim light I made out a cider bottle and an empty beer can lying on a cubicle floor.

'It's a dump,' said the Welshman. 'Why don't you go to the Night Shelter down St Pancras Way? You get three nights free down there, and as much fucking toast and marmalade as you can eat. Tea and soup as well, all free. I'm going down Thursday.'

At 10.30, I joined about thirty men on the stairs leading to the bedrooms. Many leaned against the tiled walls, barely able to stand. I could see an iron gate at the top of the first flight of stairs, a gate which was locked. Another barrier, I thought. What function did it serve?

'It's ridiculous,' said an Irishman on the first landing. 'Two million quid and what have they got to show? Those new boilers, for a start. I bet they never even turn them on when they're in.'

The man standing next to him nodded. He said: 'Have you seen those bloody turnstiles, the new ones? Do you know how much they cost? Two fucking thousand pounds. It's bloody criminal, they don't even need them. The Salvation Army manages OK without them.'

'You'll never change them,' said a wise old man. 'They just do things for show. The system will never change.'

I heard the iron gate being unlocked. I felt like a prisoner conspiring with my guards, someone consenting to be locked up. The line began to move forward past a man in casual clothes who stood sentry by the gate. Several men ahead of me showed him their bed tickets as they passed, but always from a distance, as a token gesture. He nodded, but stopped no one. I passed by, too, a newcomer, a person worth checking, but he did not examine my ticket. I tried to work out in my own mind what function the gate was intended to serve. If it was to make sure that only those with tickets had been allowed up, why had there been no scrutiny? And if there was no scrutiny, why have gates at all? It seemed to be a meaningless ritual. But perhaps it had another purpose – to keep us in our place. I felt humiliated to have to queue to go to bed. I had been kept waiting, I had been obliged to pass through a barrier, I had been noted by Authority. Perhaps that was the whole point.

My cubicle was a tiny open-topped cell on the second floor, one of more than a hundred in a maze of corridors and fire doors. The side-walls were painted cream and seemed to be made of metal. The bed was a three-inch mattress on a plywood base, the sheets newly washed but grey with the sweat of years. There were two blankets, and there seemed to be no heating.

I could see the urine in the corridor outside, and I wondered where the lavatories were. I had seen only one on my floor. It was by the stairs, and a long walk off. The punk whom I had seen unconscious in the dining hall was talking to a friend in the corridor outside my door.

'I was fucking sitting there at lunchtime,' he said. 'Next thing I know it's half past fucking ten tonight.'

I hung my clothes on the chair by my bed, not risking my belongings too near the corridor, within reach of someone climbing over the top of the cubicle wall. I bolted the door. The temperature dropped quickly in the night, and I had to breathe under the blankets to give myself warmth. The light in the corridor outside shone directly in my face, and I woke twice, thinking it was already day. At eight o'clock a handbell sounded some way off, getting closer and closer until it was right outside my door. The noise was deafening. I dressed and made my way downstairs.

In the corridor were bundles of dirty sheets, most of which smelt of urine. At the iron gate I stopped to examine a fire door which seemed to lead to a fire escape on the outside of the building. There was a padlock and chain, firmly tying the doors in place, and a notice which read: 'Notify Front Office Before Opening This Door.' I recalled a statement from a local official claiming that all the padlocks on fire doors had been removed. But all inspection of the building was done by the same authority – and who in the outside world was to know what reforms had been carried out and which neglected?

Downstairs, in the corridor off the dining hall, I found a fire notice printed in red.

'Number One,' it said, 'raise the alarm.' Someone had added – 'then run like hell'.

The punk was in the breakfast queue with his friends. A lank-haired youth said: 'Sid's into the needle as well, now.' He laughed, as if he had told a joke.

A balding man said: 'I fucking hate pheno-fucking-barbitone. I fucking hate it.'

It was a long line to the breakfast hatch, and no one seemed to be in a hurry. Many of the men were old and infirm, sinking into desperation; some, like the punk and his friends, were young and cocky, men who pretended they had cracked the system.

'No cereal, only porridge,' said the pasty-faced woman behind the hatch. She gave me a bowl of sickly-sweet porridge, a cup of sugared tea, and a plate containing a cold fried egg and a sausage. She picked up two slices of bread and margarine in her hands and deposited them on the plate.

'That'll be forty pence,' she said.

'Have you got a tray?' I asked.

'No,' she said, 'you'll have to put your tea on your plate, dear.'

I ferried the food to the nearest empty table, spilling the milk from the porridge on the floor. I found the porridge too sweet to eat, and confined my breakfast to the sausage and the cup of tea.

'See you on Thursday,' said the Welshman I had met the night before. 'You remember where it is, don't you? The Night Shelter, St Pancras Way. And you won't have any bother getting in either, you're a first-timer, see. You'll be able to walk straight in. As much toast and fucking jam as you can eat and you won't spend a penny.' I said I would see him there. I walked up Southampton Row towards Euston. In the morning rush-hour, a pretty girl in pink trousers and an expensive trench-coat stood in the centre of the pavement reading a newspaper, apparently oblivious of the bustle around her. She looked up briefly and recoiled in horror as she saw me walking towards her. She packed up her newspaper and hurried out of my way. I felt as though I had committed an indecent assault.

Later that day, I realized my true potential for terror. It began with a ride on the Underground trains. They were warm, and I needed no excuse to sit in comfort for long periods of time. I embarked at Baker Street with a ticket for Euston Square, two stops up the line. I intended to make several circuits of the Circle Line before I got off, and to use the time to write my diary. The reaction of the other travellers was predictable at first – smart businessmen looked down their noses, students giggled. But at one station I noticed a girl in her early twenties who seemed to be thrown into a state of panic by my presence. I had stepped out of the train for a breath of fresh air when she arrived on the platform. She was blonde and pretty, carrying a small suitcase. The platform was crowded, but she kept looking nervously towards me, a quick turn of her head every few seconds, like a bird watching a cat. She seemed to expect an attack at any second, and whenever I returned her glance, her panic increased.

On the train she sat close to a black girl on the opposite side of the carriage to me. But my presence in the confined space only seemed to increase her terror. She began to tap her high-heeled boots on the floor, like a child who wants to use the lavatory. She looked towards the black girl for protection.

'Can you tell me if this is the station I should get off at?' she asked, showing her a street map. The look on her face said: 'Please help me.'

The black girl sensed that something was wrong and glanced at me. She understood, but she could not help.

'I'm afraid you're two stops after me,' she whispered.

The blonde girl's boots began to tap more rapidly. Two stops later, the black girl got off, and the stop after that I could stand it no longer. The girl was in such a state of terror that I felt I had to leave the train before we reached her stop. She gasped as I stood up, and when I disembarked I saw her scurrying along the carriage, where she struck up a conversation with a safe-looking middle-aged man.

I felt ashamed that my appearance had caused someone such pain. I had wanted to apologize to her in some way, but I knew that any approach I could have made would only have increased her panic.

That night I slept in a cramped hut under a railway bridge near Broad Street Station. It was a motor repair yard called Bow Wow's, a residence for waifs and strays run by a second-hand mobile-home salesman. He showed me into the men's dormitory, a room some 12 feet by 14, containing nine beds stacked three bunks high. Next door were the women's quarters with fifteen beds, again in three-tier bunks. He was smartly dressed; he might have been an off-duty policeman.

'It's two pounds fifty,' he said. 'It's pretty rough and ready, but it'll do for you for . . . you've got showers over there and a TV room. You don't get breakfast, not for two pounds fifty in London, you know that. Are you signing on or anything?'

'Well . . .'

'The reason I ask is because we've got a pretty good relationship with the DHSS and if you want a chit from us tomorrow morning to say that you stayed here, you can take it down, and they'll issue you with a Giro.'

He showed me the shower room, which was across a yard crowded with motor caravans, old tyres and huge diesel engines. There was a building like a public lavatory which contained showers, lavatories and urinals and seemed to be reasonably clean.

'The only thing,' he said, 'I don't want to be authoritarian, the only thing we don't have here is we don't have people going out and getting pissed out of their mind and then coming in. The rest of it, there's no restrictions, you just come and go as you like.'

His clientele seemed young, most were in their late teens or early twenties, and many were simple-minded. I counted seven men and three women, most of whom were in a separate hut watching a television programme about the British Motor Show. An overweight girl with thick pebble glasses lay on a sofa, her hands inside the waistband of her skirt. The commentator said:

'In Japan, only three cars in every one hundred are imported.'
We saw pictures of Japanese workers making cars.

'Ha, soh,' said a skinhead youth with dangling braces. 'Velly glud Chinese takeaway.'

He looked around his companions and a mongoloid youth on the plastic bench seat behind him smiled broadly, his eyes almost disappearing among the folds of loose skin. The others continued to watch the screen, stony-faced.

'One of the more interested visitors to this year's Motor Show,' said the commentator, 'is this man, Lewis Collins, better known as Bodie of *The Professionals*. He likes to drive fast not only on the screen, but also in real life. In fact, he does all his own driving stunts on the show. So we gave him something a little special to try out . . . a Porsche 928.'

There was a helicopter's-eye view of a sleek silver Porsche car accelerating round a steeply banked corner on a racing track. In the background, the signature tune of the current *Boys Own* spy serial began to pulse.

The two skinheads on the bench seat began to squirm with excitement.

'Fucking hell!' said one.

'Fuck me!' said the other.

Bodie looked cool behind the wheel, the slightest hint of a smile playing about his pouting lips.

'Just testing the acceleration now,' he told us. 'Mmmmm . . . not bad. Not as much as I'd expected, but not bad.'

The car roared away, then came to a snaking halt.

'Fucking Jesus,' said the first skinhead.

'Great!' said the other.

Bodie showed us the engine.

'Very small for a V-8,' he said. One of the skinheads nodded, sagely. 'But it packs a punch – two hundred and forty brake horsepower.'

'Two hundred and forty!' said the second skinhead.

I looked through the window of the hut to the yard outside. It was raining, and the water dripped off the railway bridge on to a pile of tyres. It had soaked the mats that the owner had put down to stop dirt being trailed around the yard. Most of the motor caravans were bumper to bumper – until recently they,

84

too, had been used as housing for the homeless, and a notice under the television warned residents not to smoke in their vans.

'You'll have to pay a little extra for my special paint job,' said Bodie, standing by his Porsche. He chuckled. 'Anyone got twenty-five thousand quid?'

'Jesus fucking Christ!' said the first skinhead.

'Fucking hell!' said the second.

'Did you hear that? Twenty-five fucking thousand.'

The whole assembly sat open-mouthed. They grinned at each other. One of the skinheads jumped up in his seat, causing his braces to fly into the air.

'I want a car that does two thousand miles an hour!' he said, skimming his hand in front of his nose. *'Vrooommph!'*

The programme showed Ford executives planning their strategy for the Motor Show. Smart-suited men were moving model cars around a model exhibition stand.

'Ha, look at 'im,' said the first skinhead, 'playing with toy fucking cars!' Everyone laughed.

I got up to leave, passing the fat girl in the doorway. She looked at me suspiciously; with my unshaven face and my torn coat, I was far worse dressed than any of the others. She put her hands inside the elasticated waistband of her skirt and hurried by.

It rained heavily that night, and I lay on my bunk listening to the scampering drops on the roof above. I wondered how loud it must sound to the boy in the top bunk. He had not been in the television hut with the rest, he was well-dressed and apparently very shy. He might almost have worked in a bank. Why, I wondered, was he there, in the damp darkness under a railway bridge?

By eight the following morning it seemed too dark to be day. I wondered if my watch was still working. Outside, several streets were under water and the traffic had slowed to a crawl. I left through the wicket gate of the motor repair yard. As I passed the office for the last time, I noticed a sticker on the window urging me to join the Automobile Association. Outside was a sign advertising the sale of motor caravans, and I saw an old man whose trailer was parked near by going into the yard to use the washroom.

It was rush-hour in the café near the station, and office workers in damp clothes were crowded together, spinning out the last moments before they had to make a dash for it. There was one seat free in the corner, and I sat down next to a man reading his morning paper. He had the air of someone who rarely disobeyed. He buttocked his way a few inches along the seat, and angled his paper towards me, so that his face was hidden from mine. After a few minutes, he put down the paper with a flurry, drank the last dregs of his tea as though he were competing in a drinking marathon, and then stood up hurriedly.

'Sorry,' he said, pushing past me.

The man opposite also got up to go, leaving a nervous-looking man in a car-coat who watched me as I took another huge bite from my hamburger. He shuffled across to another table.

I sat alone in the bandstand of Finsbury Circus on a folding green chair more normally reserved for members of the bowling club. I was hidden from view by a stack of similar chairs which had been placed in the bandstand to keep them out of the rain. In front of me, the bowling green was half-submerged in water, a lush spontaneous lake reflecting the trees and the office buildings beyond.

I could hear the swish of the traffic in the distance. On the green, several pigeons squished their way along in the sodden turf. Raincoated men climbed the steps of the bandstand to get a better view of the flooding as they made their way to work. Many of them did not notice me in the gloom, but one of them turned and gave me a polite 'Good morning!' I returned his greeting, but he was already moving on.

I sat for an hour, breathing in the fresh scent of the park in the rain; then I folded my green chair and returned it to the stack.

'When shall we three meet again? In thunder, lightning or in rain?'

It was an Irish voice under a trilby hat, and there were nearer thirty of us than three.

'When the hurlyburly's done, when the battle's lost and won. That will be ere the set of the sun,' he said, rattling off the lines with relish. 'Where's the place? Upon the heath. There to meet with Macbeth. What do you fancy for the Dewhurst Stakes at Newmarket? Storm Bird is a powerful good runner.'

There was silence from the others.

'I'd fancy Storm Bird against all the rest, myself,' said the Trilby.

Thirty men, huddled on the steps of an old mansion. There was wire mesh on one of the windows, and the porchway was a makeshift affair of corrugated iron and scaffolding. In its day, it had housed grand people; now it was the Hobo's Hilton, the Night Shelter. It was ten in the evening, and the front door was about to open for the first time. Some of the men had been waiting for five hours.

'I think Centurius stands a fair old chance,' said another Irish voice from the centre of the pack.

'No, no,' said the Trilby, 'not now O'Brien's got Eddery riding for him. And you must not forget that Storm Bird's father was Northern Dancer, the same horse that sired Nijinsky, The Minstrel and Try My Best.'

There was a reverend silence.

'What is the Christian name of Lester Piggott's father?' said a snub-nosed man who was staring aggressively at the Trilby.

'It's Keith, Keith Piggott.'

'No, you're wrong. Keith is the brother.'

'No,' said the Trilby. 'Keith is the father, the brother is a farmer who you don't hear much of.'

'And when was Lester Piggott born?'

'The fifth of November 1936, at Wantage in Berkshire,' said the Trilby.

'Yes, you're right there, your man is forty-four years old.'

They were thoroughbreds both, a race of champions on the course of courses, and we dray-horses could only grind our bits in wonder. The trilby hat tilted upwards.

'The American horse, of course, is by far the superior beast. They're congenitally hardier because they're raced so often. Your British or French horse is lucky if he has three or four races a season.'

He told us that the Curragh was the best race-course in the world, and that the clever rider should take the outside to get the full advantage of the camber. He told us that Lester Piggott drank a special bitter brew of coffee that had to be made a particular way, and that he knew that way. It was an endless stream of racing consciousness that flowed and rippled over our pebble brains, a freshet, a swollen beck that swept us along like trout in the sunshine of pure wisdom.

'I've only had two and a half pints,' said a drunk to my left. He began to sway.

A car drew up, an old Austin 1100. A shabby old man struggled out of the driving seat and started walking towards us. As one, thirty angry faces turned towards him.

'Surely to God they're not turning up in cars now,' said the Trilby, 'and with us dossers all on foot.'

There was a stretched silence as the old man mounted the pavement.

'Can you tell me the way to Euston Station?' he said. There was a humming noise, as thirty pairs of lungs exhaled. The old man was no threat to our chances of a bed that night.

'Turn left, then right and right again,' said a man from the back with exaggerated cheerfulness.

'Thanks, thank you,' said the old man.

'If he says I'm drunk, he's wrong,' said the man in the checked coat to my left.

The black door opened and a man in his early thirties, dressed like a lumberjack, stood in the doorway.

'Those who were here last night,' he shouted.

A group of about ten men began to push forward – the others stood aside. I watched them give their names to the man on the door, while he ticked them off on a list. The Welshman whom I had met in Bruce House was pressed up against the entrance, gesticulating in my direction.

'You're a first-timer, aren't you?' he said.

'Er . . . yes.'

'Well, you should be in front of this fucking lot, by rights. Let him come forward.'

Several men in front of me turned round to see who he was talking to, but none of them broke ranks.

'I'm all right,' I said.

The man in the checked raincoat seemed to be arguing with the doorman, both men raising their hands. Then he rushed down the steps, red-faced, and disappeared into the gloom.

'Drunk,' said the man in front of me.

'He shouldn't have had it,' said an educated voice. I turned to see a man with a nut-brown face, bald, with the appearance of a tortoise. 'They can smell it,' he said, 'even the slightest amount.'

The black door closed, leaving about twenty of us on the step. We waited another ten minutes. There was no conversation, and I wondered how many of us would be turned away. The lumberjack appeared again, and invited us all to step forward. He asked me my name, and inquired if I had stayed before.

'No,' I said.

'Well, just stand over there in the hallway with that other chap, and I'll see you in a minute.'

The other chap was a grizzled Irishman in his late thirties, a shy man who looked like a mongrel dog which had grown used to being beaten. His body seemed to shrink against the wall, as if he were trying to make himself inconspicuous.

'Your first time too?' I said.

He nodded.

The lumberjack approached us, clipboard in hand.

'Right,' he said, 'let me tell you what's what. You get three nights, OK, but you must take them in a row, there's no one night here and two nights later on, OK?'

We both nodded.

'There's a shower, wash-basins and toilets through there, if you want to clean up, OK?'

Another nod.

'You can get a towel from the office round the corner. Downstairs, through that door, is the kitchen, and you can help yourself to anything in there. There are no women tonight, so you can sleep in the women's room. Just take any bed that's not been made up, all right, and take as many blankets as you can find. Oh yes, and no drink is allowed in the hostel. If you even smell of drink when you come in tomorrow, even if you've only had a pint, you won't be allowed in, OK?'

Our room was large, about twenty feet square. It might once have been a dining room or a second lounge. The walls had been scraped bare, and a cheap curtain hung at the rear window. Through the dark glass I could make out a small garden backing on to a tall brick wall. Our beds were canvas camp beds, with pillows coated in a shiny white plastic which felt cold to the touch. We each had four blankets.

'It's all right,' said the Irishman.

'Yeah, great.'

We went down to the kitchen in the basement. There was a smell of toast, and a roar of conversation like that in a pub. About twenty men were crowded round four tables; others were cooking toast on a grill in the corner, or pouring tea from a large urn. The cauldron on the stove was empty, the remains of a thick soup visible as a thin film on the bottom.

The Welshman said: 'The buggers have finished off the bloody lot, them that was in first. How many were there? About ten, was it? Someone must have taken a fucking bucketful up to his room.'

His voice had the boom of the poet, a Sunday-best voice, full of *mawr*, majesty. It made the meanness of sentiment smaller by contrast.

'Sit down there, boy,' he said, indicating a spare seat at the table. 'See, I didn't tell you wrong now, did I? As much fucking toast and jam as you can eat. Help yourself, don't be fucking shy.'

I sat next to a man who told me he was from the heart of Irish racing country, a pear-shaped young fellow with rosy cheeks.

'I'm from racing country as well,' I said. 'Doncaster.'

He looked not one jot impressed.

'Ah, a great course, Doncaster,' he said, 'but I had no luck there myself. I backed three or four horses at nine to one, but they all lost. I came out about three hundred pounds down in all.'

I looked disbelieving. 'How much did you bet each time?' I asked.

'Oh, about thirty pounds,' he said. 'Pity none of it did me the slightest good.'

'And how did you afford that?' I asked.

'Oh, I do bits of work here and there,' he said. 'I'm working on a conversion job at the moment, some flats. That's saved me a bob or two, I can tell you. We slept in the place last night, me and a mate. Mind you, we had to be pretty quiet about it, there were people still living in the flat below, and they'd have called the fucking police straight away if they'd heard anything, I'm sure of that.'

The well-spoken man sat opposite. He looked as if he had just returned from a holiday in the Mediterranean. His bald head shone with brownness, like a bronze bust, an impression heightened by the aquilinity of his nose. He looked like a Roman emperor.

'You should go to Germany,' he told me. 'Lot of call for painters and decorators out there. You could earn two hundred and fifty pounds a week quite easily, and the accommodation is cheap. I know, I used to live there myself.'

His accent seemed to jar with the other men; he was distrusted, not least for his appearance. He was the only man in the room with a three-piece suit on, for a start. I saw the Welshman's eyes look to the ceiling in an expression which said: 'Bloody know-all!'

'They serve beer instead of tea on all the building sites in Germany,' said the Emperor, 'and if you get stuck for accommodation, there's none of this nonsense about the police moving you on at railway stations. But you should have no trouble finding accommodation in the first place.'

I found his knowledge of sleeping in stations totally at odds with his delivery. It was like a road sweeper knowing about claret.

'It's true about the painting and decorating,' said the Irishman. 'They want men with skills everywhere in Germany. You should have no trouble in London for that matter, either.'

I was surprised that no one argued against the idea of getting a job, and I felt the incongruity of talking about salaries more than double the national average wage, when we were in a Night Shelter for the destitute. Were these men lying when they claimed first-hand experience of salaries of more than £200 a week, or had the jobs they talked about been so short-lived that they were regarded as a windfall, an interlude in their persistent poverty? Perhaps, I thought, the truth was that such jobs did exist, but that none of these men had ever risked taking one.

There were only half a dozen men left in the kitchen by eleven o'clock, most of the bread having been eaten and the tea in the urn having been drunk to the bitter dregs. A young black man was standing by the sink, wearing a black gaberdine coat and a flat hat, even though the temperature was high. His movements were convulsive, violent, as though an earthquake was erupting deep inside him. He tried to disguise the spasms by turning the movement into something which looked intentional. He spun round as though he were dancing, trying at the same time to balance his mug and plate. It was like watching a juggler in a circus: an unending series of movements, each bringing him to the brink of disaster yet never quite toppling him over the edge.

A mouse-like man skipped round him as if he were avoiding a poisonous snake.

'What fucking room's he in?' he said, leaping to one side as the black man's dance whirled nearer. 'Because I'm not sleeping with filth like that.'

The black man's eyes rolled, and he jerked convulsively away into the corner, where he tried to stay still, eating his toast. The eruptions continued, and he stood like a man wrestling with an imaginary wild beast.

In the far corner, I heard a man who looked like an unsuccessful encyclopedia salesman boasting about how much money he had earned in recent jobs.

'I don't mind paying fifty quid a week for a hotel, when I'm in work,' he said, munching a slice of toast. 'But for that sort of money I insist on getting something for it; my own room, and somewhere to wash. I mean, the point is, if you're not getting that, why bother? This'll do me for the time being.'

I went up to the women's room, where the frightened Irishman was already in bed. There was no heating, so I lay one of my blankets on the canvas to prevent the cold rising from the floor. The Irishman was wrestling with his plastic pillow, which kept skidding on to the floor behind him.

'Where's the light switch?' I asked him.

'I don't think there is one,' he said. 'They must switch it off for us.'

I washed in the room next door, then I undressed in the women's room, placing my coat on top of the blankets. Shortly after eleven o'clock the light was turned out. My companion turned over, careful not to lose any of the blankets he had so carefully laid. His plastic pillow slithered once more to the ground. During the course of the night, he lost it another three times.

'You know, this fucking city's impossible, it's too bloody big,' said the encyclopedia salesman at breakfast. 'I was trying to get somewhere at half past seven this morning, now it looks like being half past eight if I'm lucky, which I'm not. It's bloody impossible to keep appointments, you know that?'

I distrusted him. Somehow his crumpled grey suit and his neatly combed hair made his talk of an appointment all the more implausible. The man seemed one big excuse.

'I had this casual job a few months ago,' he told me, 'and it finished. It would have been a good job too. The fella told me to clean the ovens, which was fair enough, but there was this young bloke there, an Englishman, who looked as if he hadn't been in the place five minutes, and he's walking around like he owned the fucking place. So I said to him: give us a hand with these ovens since you're not doing anything, which he wasn't, and he said: sorry, but he worked for the company and the ovens weren't the company's responsibility. Do you like that?'

He told me he had been dismissed the following day, and that the boss had shown clear favouritism. He took another big bite on his toast and marmalade, keeping an eye on his tea at the same time.

'You know,' he said, sipping from the plastic mug, 'there was a time when I held jobs for six or seven months. It's easy once you've passed the first month. A little determination can take you a long way. But these days, I find it hard to stick it out more than a day or two.'

He looked at the edge of his toast as if it were the only friend he had in the world. He told me another story of how he had been dismissed from a hotel near Regent's Park, only this time the man who had been idling while he had been working was a black man.

'That's your fucking darkies for you,' said the mouse-like man from the far side of the room. He was looking directly at the black man who suffered from spasms. The black glanced at me, then spun away to the corner near the stove. It was as though I was threatening him too.

'Those bastards hold all the aces,' said the encyclopedia salesman. 'As soon as they know you've been sent by Mortimer Street, they treat you like dirt. They know they can just get rid of you, no questions asked.'

He was referring to the government job agency for the casual trade in Mortimer Street – a place well known to most people round the table.

The warden of the Night Shelter, still dressed like a lumberjack, appeared in the kitchen doorway.

'Closing here in five minutes,' he said.

'I think he's in a bigger hurry than I am,' said the salesman. 'Your man looks soft, but he's hard, bloody hard.'

He began to butter some toast with an energy I had not seen him use all morning.

The Welshman pressed me to have more toast, but I told him I had eaten enough.

'Well, if you get hungry later,' he said, 'there's the Simon up the road, that's open from ten in the morning until one. You can get some bread and tea there, as much as you want. Then you can go again at five and have some more, and they'll let you watch the telly until about nine. Then it's nearly time to come back here for ten.'

'And what are you going to do today?' I asked him.

'Oh,' he said, with a glint in his eye, 'I'll know that when I step outside the door.'

I walked to Waterloo, a distance of some three or four miles, hoping to eat in the same Spanish café I had found at the weekend. It meant hanging about the station for a few hours, but I was getting used to that. Waterloo Station was much more crowded than I'd remembered it, thousands of people milling in the concourse, jostling for position as they scuttled to and from the platforms. I sat on a bench seat near the bookstall. It had been moved since my previous visit six days before to make way for workmen installing screens and barriers. One man was drilling into the newly laid concrete, another was ferrying loads of paving slabs with a fork-lift truck.

Beside me was a one-legged old man in clothes even shabbier than my own. His crutches lay by his side, together with three or four plastic carrier-bags which seemed to be filled with old clothes. Another dosser joined us, a stocky man with wild curly hair and a skin so blackened he might have spent the night in a coal cellar. Even his bald patch was dark, like cow-hide.

We had been sitting for about a quarter of an hour, watching the men at work, when a policeman approached us.

'Right,' he said, looking at us each in turn, 'on your way.'

The blackened man started to gather his belongings. I looked at the policeman quizzically.

'Are you travelling anywhere?' he asked.

'Yes,' I said. 'I'm just waiting for a friend to come, then we'll be on our way.'

It was true. I had an appointment with the film crew, who had arranged to meet me there.

'I mean,' said the policeman with infinite patience, 'are you travelling on a train?'

'No,' I said.

'Well, in that case, you're not entitled to sit there. That seat is reserved for the travelling public.'

'But I've arranged to meet my friend here,' I said.

'Look, I don't want any talk,' said the policeman becoming agitated. 'Either you move or I nick you, all right?'

The two other dossers had already packed their bags and were beginning to move away. They had said nothing during this exchange, and looked vaguely embarrassed by my apparent stupidity. I stood up, and walked over to the bookstall, where I began to look at some magazines. The policeman watched me, satisfying himself that I had no immediate intention of resuming my seat, and then he walked away into the crowd.

The one-legged man limped after him on crutches. My other companion had quietly sat down on another bench, out of view. I waited a few minutes in the bookstall, then I resumed my seat. Next to me was an old man who told me he was staying at the Salvation Army hostel in Blackfriars Road near by. I began to wonder if any of the seats were occupied by travellers at all.

He said the Salvation Army was quite strict – if you even

smelt of drink, they threw you out. But, he said, they did not shove religion down his throat, a fact for which he was grateful.

'A man tried to sell me his meal ticket the other day,' he said. 'He wanted to buy a bottle of cider. I told him I wasn't having anything of that, because his ticket had his name and his bed number on it, and I'd have been out on my ear if they'd found out.'

His accent sounded like those I had heard in Suffolk, and I asked him if he was from those parts.

'No, I'm not from Suffolk, you've got the wrong bloke,' he shouted, as if I had accused him of a crime. 'I'm from St Albans, Hurts, you understand? St Albans, Hurts.' His voice was getting louder, and he pronounced the name of the county as it was spelt. 'ST ALBANS HURTS,' he continued, 'ST A – L – B – A – N – S H – E – R – T – S. ST ALBANS HURTS!' He was at screaming pitch, and his voice echoed round the girders above our heads. Scores of people looked round to see what was happening. They glared at me as if I had tried to rob the old man.

I tried to calm him down, but it was several minutes before he regained his composure. He told me he was sixty-two, and he gave me the exact address of his birthplace in St Albans as though he were filling in yet another government form.

'I go back to St Albans every Thursday on the train,' he said. 'But there's nowhere to stay in St Albans. There's no Salvation Army hostel like here.'

I decided to get weighed. It had been ten days since I took to the streets, and my diet had changed dramatically. I wanted to find out if the high fat content of my meals had altered my weight, or if all the walking I was doing had counterbalanced the higher carbohydrate intake. I went down into the Gents in the basement, where I found a large red weighing machine with a huge circular dial, like the ones I had stepped on at the seaside when I was small.

I took off my heavy overcoat, and laid it on a shoe-shining machine, then I placed my bag and my radio on the floor. The machine took a 5 pence piece. The needle registered 10 stones, 7 pounds, exactly the same weight as when I had set out. I

'How could the destitute be punished more than they punish themselves?'
Photo: Roger Jones

'A small frightened man with a large white suitcase'
Photo: Alex Hansen

Charing Cross arches:
'"I believe the angels are all around here," he said'
Photo: Alex Hansen

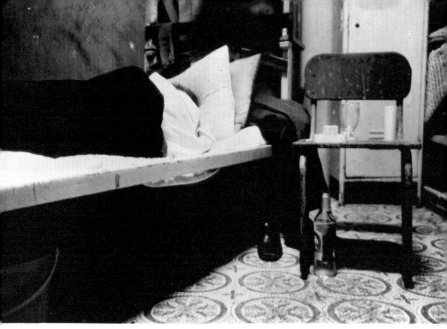

Tower Bridge Hotel:
'It was a former public house which now catered for a more serious drinking clientele'
Photo: Alex Hansen

'I tried to say: "I am human like you"'   Photo: Alex Hansen

The Tooley Hotel:
'A place that made no concessions to the soft-furnishing side of human nature'
Photo: Alex Hansen

Bruce House:
'I could not comprehend men who risked other people's lives for administrative convenience'

Photo: Alex Hansen

Bruce House:
'I felt like a prisoner conspiring with my guards'   Photo: Alex Hansen

The Spike:
'I thought it would be a hostel, I did not bargain on the Workhouse'
Photo: Alex Hansen

The Spike:
'I felt I had taken the Queen's shilling and forfeited the right to be treated as an ordinary citizen'   Photo: Alex Hansen

'The joy of getting steamed, of fouling your bed and lying in it too'
Photo: Roger Jones

Bruce House:
'All the tables and chairs had been cleared away around him'
Photo: Alex Hansen

The Spike:
'I decided not to undress in case he was right about the others stealing my
clothes'   Photo: Alex Hansen

stepped off the machine, smiling, pleased that I had at least managed to keep my weight up in spite of my reduced circumstances. I bent to pick up my coat from the shoe-shine machine, when I became aware of a young man approaching me rapidly from behind. He was smartly dressed, in his early twenties, and as he drew level with me he thrust out an arm as if he were about to seize my coat. I jumped back in surprise, and I saw his hand dart towards a folder which was propped up on the shoe-shining machine against the wall. I had not noticed it before, and it struck me that he must have thought that I had been trying to steal it. He stared at me aggressively, and I thought he was going to speak, but he tucked the folder under his arm and hurried away, bounding up the stairs two at a time.

I left Waterloo Station and walked to the Victoria Embankment where I joined the lunchtime strollers in the park. A Scotsman in a kilt, his hair tied up in a pony tail, was walking a tiny dog, striding out, oblivious to the wry smiles he left in his wake. A decrepit old gardener was sweeping leaves from under a tree one at a time, more a caress than a business-like attempt to clear the debris. I wondered if he would manage to uncover the lawn before the tree shed its next leaves. On a park bench two skinheads were eating fish and chips, feeding tit-bits to the pigeons. One of them was clearly frightened of the birds, and from time to time he leaped on to the bench itself to avoid them as they crowded round his friend's feet. He continued to feed them, however, making sure he was at a safe height.

I walked into Soho to see if the traders in Berwick Street Market would give me any of the fruit they considered unfit for sale. As I walked through the streets, the pictures of naked women in the shop windows surprised me. How many times, I wondered, had I walked through these streets and considered them merely colourful, amusing. Now they seemed almost threatening. Berwick Street was busy, working wives laden with their lunchtime shopping, buying pounds of this, half pounds of that. Could I, I thought, afford to buy fruit on my budget? I looked hard at the prices. One apple would cost me around 8 pence, a large orange nearer 12 pence. The doctor had advised me against salads, because, he said, I stood a greater risk of catching typhoid or a similar disease from foods which might have been in contact with flies. But, in the cold weather, that possibility seemed greatly lessened. He had told me to look for foods with high carbohydrate and high fat, for energy. Still, a free apple or orange would not hurt, I thought, as a supplement to all the junk food. I found a crate on a barrow which contained abandoned fruit from one of the near-by stalls. There were three oranges with the beginnings of mould on one side, several mouldy bunches of grapes, each with good fruit among the bad, and a bag of reject figs. I took an orange and popped it in my bag.

That evening, I saw the black man from the Night Shelter leaving the St Pancras Library ahead of me. It was eight o'clock, the time the library closed, and two hours before the Night Shelter opened. I followed him to St Pancras Station, where he sat on the platform, pretending to be another of the many passengers waiting for trains. His body was constantly in motion even now, trying to suppress the convulsions which seized it every few seconds.

It was a bitterly cold night, and behind him was the warmth of the buffet bar, but I guessed he dared not risk sitting at one of the tables for fear of ejection. He would not have been able to afford the price of many cups of tea, and his affliction would have drawn attention to his continued presence. I watched him from the buffet, and when he stood up from his seat, I followed. He took a route, unfamiliar to me, out of the station, and I lost sight of him for several minutes, but I knew which way he was heading. I saw him further down the road, and I walked quickly to catch up with him.

'Hello,' I said, drawing level.

He looked at me from the corner of his eye, as if afraid to turn his head fully. His body twisted and turned as he walked, causing passers-by to stop and stare. Many seemed to think he was drunk. His pace was much slower than my own, and he weaved a zig-zag course, making our conversation difficult.

'How was your room last night?' I asked him.

'O – o – o . . . All right,' he said, forcing himself to speak.

'Was it cold?'

He tried to reply, summoning up the words from the depths of his body. No speech came, and I tried again.

'My room was freezing, was yours?'

He grimaced in an effort to reply. In the silence which followed, he seemed to be trying to throw the words from his lips like a shot-putter hurling a weight. After the first attempt, he suddenly stopped writhing, and his body went limp, defeated. He tried again. This time speech bubbled to the surface, a staccato rush of words.

'My room was very cold . . . yyyy – yes.' He smiled, in triumph.

His accent seemed African, and I was about to ask him where he came from when we crossed the road into St Pancras Way and into view of the men outside the Night Shelter. It seemed cruel to let the men outside the hostel see his difficulty in trying to speak, and we ended our conversation.

There were fewer men on the steps than the night before; all of them looked hard at the African as we approached. I maintained the pace of my companion, but he sensed trouble and held back by the railings as we drew near.

'It must have been a fucking good pay-day today,' said a snub-nosed man I had seen the night before. 'I've never seen it so quiet.'

'I went to St Mungo's last night,' said a young Scot. 'Fucking great it is in there. You can doss doon all fucking day if you like. If you're not in work that day, they let you flake oot, nae bother.'

He wore a suit, the jacket collar turned up against the cold. I was surprised how few of the men wore coats; many were shivering, their teeth chattering loudly. Near the door, I saw a black-haired man who had not been with us the previous night. His nose was squashed like a boxer's, and he looked as if he had just been in a bad fight. Both nostrils were filled with clotted blood, forcing him to breathe through his mouth. His eyes were badly blackened, the bruises spreading right down his cheeks to his mouth. He spoke to no one.

At five minutes to ten, a fresh-faced youth arrived at the back of the group and asked to be allowed through. He seemed polite and well-spoken, and a couple of men made as though to push him back. The others, however, stood aside to let him through.

'He's usually here before this,' said the Welshman. 'Very

unusual, that is. Wonder who else is on tonight?' He looked through the wire mesh on the front office window and made out the form of a girl.

'Oh, she's on, the girl. That's all right, then. Better than that other bloke, he doesn't let you get away with a thing.'

The young warden came to the door, holding a clipboard. In a voice barely audible he said: 'Last night.'

All the men who had stayed the previous night, including me, came forward. I was sixth in line.

'Name?'

'Crabbe,' I said.

'Tony?'

'Yeah.'

He ticked me off his list and I went inside. This time I was determined to go straight to the kitchen, before the soup had all been eaten. The Welshman was already on his way down the wooden staircase to the cellar.

'Come on,' he urged, 'no time to fucking lose.'

He told the Mongrel, who had slept with me in the women's room the night before, to follow suit, and we bounded down the staircase, two steps at a time. We had each drunk a bowl of mixed vegetable soup before most of the others had even arrived. The Welshman kept piling slice after slice of Sunblest bread on to my plate.

'Come on, plenty more where that came from,' he said. 'Get fucking stuck in.'

I asked him where he had been during the day, and he told me he had been walking around.

'I been at the Simon this evening,' he said. 'Eight fucking cups of soup, nine fucking slices and potatoes, boiled and baked, and as much fucking tea as I could drink. You know, a woman stopped me in the street in Camden today and pinched my fucking cheek. She said: how you getting so fat? I said by fucking signing on, didn't I?'

He helped himself to more bread and jam. I found his appetite quite daunting. The African sat next to me and tried to prepare himself some bread and jam. His spoon flew over the table like a child's model aeroplane, swooping down near the jam dish in an attempt to scoop enough out to spread on his bread. The

Welshman watched in horror as the first and second attempts failed. He pushed the jam dish and the butter dish towards the African's end of the table.

'Here,' he said, 'take the fucking lot for fuck's sake.'

The African scooped a spoonful of jam, jerked it into the air and deposited it on the floor near my feet.

'For crying out fucking loud,' said the Welshman.

Everyone in the room was now staring at the African as he stooped below the table to pick up the jam from the floor. He grasped the thick red jelly in his hand and carried it to the sink, where he flicked it off and washed it away. He returned to his seat and tried again. This time, he deposited a large cube of butter on a slice of bread, a blob of jam by its side, and tried to spread them both. The butter burrowed into the soft white bread, and he gave up any attempt to spread it. He folded the bread over, and began to eat. The men at the next table grinned and nudged each other.

'Whereabouts in Africa are you from?' I asked him, trying to divert attention. It had the opposite effect – the others looked at me with dismay.

'Ffffff – from the West,' he said.

'Where, Nigeria?'

'No, Gggggg – Ghana.'

Everyone was looking at us, many with a kind of horrified fascination. I decided to end the conversation for the moment. An Irishman dressed all in black, with black curly hair and a long pointed beard, strode into the room. He was tiny, like a fairy-tale goblin. He reminded me of drawings of Rumpelstiltskin I had seen when I was a child.

The Welshman pointed to him, saying: 'He had eight mugs of soup at the Simon with me, that fucker. We had a great time.'

The hobgoblin tiptoed to the soup cauldron and helped himself to his ninth mug of the evening. He was not the only fairy-tale villain in the room. There were a whole collection of trolls, wizards, big bad uncles, sprites and ogres. Many were the faces of church gargoyles, sunken noses, bulging eyes, faces with sheep's hair and eagle's beaks, faces pitted with burns or erupting with buboes, faces of desperation, faces of fear. Even the rosy-cheeked Welshman, for all his rolling-eyed gaiety, had fear lurking beneath the surface of his skin. How, I wondered, could a man as alive as he appeared to be gain so much satisfaction from a few bowls of free soup? He had won the prize, yet what had he won?

I went upstairs to the lavatory. The wall was covered in cryptic graffiti. 'Help a Drunk Today – buy him a drink,' said one. To one side, someone had written, mysteriously, 'I am Jurassic Limestone.'

My bed was next to the Emperor's. He was lying in his suit, reading an up-market collection of crime stories. In the opposite corner of the room a man was wrapping each item of clothing he took off in newspaper. He was the same man who had been so afraid of the African the night before.

'Why are you doing that?' asked his neighbour, looking at the parcels by the man's bed.

'It's to protect them from the mice,' he said.

As I undressed, a man in a vest shouted across to the Emperor: 'Who was that fucking bloke in the bed next to you last night?'

'I don't know who you're talking about,' said the Emperor, like a judge passing sentence.

'I'm glad we got shut of him. Do you know, he didn't even bother to get undressed. Just took his fucking shoes off and climbed straight into bed. Disgusting I call that.'

'I didn't notice,' said the Emperor, continuing to read his book. When he climbed into bed himself, a few minutes later, he was still wearing his shirt, socks, long johns and a vest.

> This is the Life,
> Doss, doss, doss.
> It's Great for us
> Lazy Scotch Bastards.

It was not the greatest poetry in the world, I thought, as I held the door to against the morning rush.

'Come on,' said a voice from the other side. 'Hurry up.'

It was the Mouse Man, and I was damned if I was going to hurry for him. I pushed back against the door to prevent his entering. I flushed the lavatory and walked into the back boiler room. The Mouse Man scurried past me; he looked bad-tempered and I noticed he was already wearing his overcoat. In the washroom there was soap to wash my hands, and I took advantage while I could. But, as with everywhere else I had stayed, there were no plugs in the basins. I stuffed some newspaper down the plug-hole and filled the basin with hot water. The luxury of having a clean towel was something I relished; I bathed again and again, letting the warm water redden my face in the mirror. Behind me, I could see the Mouse Man trying to hang up his overcoat. Each time he managed to get it within a few inches of the hook on the back of the door, the door opened again, and he fell back, panting.

'It's so heavy,' he said.

He began to try again, and on the third attempt he threw it over the hook.

'It's new,' he said. 'Well, new from the Church Army. I went there to find somewhere to sleep, but they couldn't help. They said I could look through their clothes store, though, so I did.'

Saturday-morning breakfast was half an hour later than on weekdays. We had all been allowed to lie in until eight o'clock. In the kitchen, a burly Cockney was launching into yet another diatribe about the scandal of the £2,000,000 being spent on Bruce House. Like most of the other critics I had heard on the subject, he was most concerned that the money was not going into his pocket.

'I could do the outside of that place for half the price they're paying,' he said. 'And it would be a proper job, stripping, sealing, two undercoats, no short-cuts.'

He broadened the subject, to take in the scandal of the money paid to staff which would be better off in the pockets of citizens like himself.

'That little chippy's getting two hundred quid a week to my certain knowledge,' he said. 'And he's never even there week-ends, but he still gets double time for Sundays and time and a half for his day off. And that woman in the kitchen gets over a hundred quid a week. I know, 'cos she lent me fifty once from her pay packet, and she still had sixty quid left.'

I had no idea if the figures he gave were fact or fiction; only the jealousy was real.

'A hundred fucking quid, eh?' said a gap-toothed Yorkshireman. 'I know what I'd do with it, straight down the bookies, twenty quid, fifty quid, crash! crash!' He thumped the table for emphasis.

The girl warden came into the kitchen and began stacking cups and plates by the sink. She seemed painfully shy, and avoided catching anyone's eye. There was an awkward silence as the men in the room followed her with their eyes. It was not that she was dressed to attract – far from it, her clothes were shabby, a dreary black and white coverall. I wondered why she did not speak, since the only way to find out about any of us was to ask questions, but she denied herself even the natural opportunities to do so. The African carried his mug and plate to the sink and offered to help her, but she said she could manage.

I waited for the African in the street outside the Night Shelter, hoping to have a long conversation with him as we walked. We set off in the direction of the Simon Community, and I was afraid he would go straight in to take advantage of the free bread and tea. I could not risk joining him there without involving myself in complicated explanations. It meant our talk had to be brief.

'How long have you had the trouble with your arms and legs?' I asked him.

'I – I j – jjjj – ust like to mm – m – move quickly,' he said. 'I roll, I roll.'

'Yes, but what happened to you, how did you get your illness?'

He zig-zagged across the pavement, and at first I thought I had pressed him too far.

Then he said: 'I – I – I – I used to have this lifting job.'

'What, in Ghana?'

He nodded.

'I got th – th – this diseeease,' he said.

He told me he had come to Britain with a Ghanaian friend, and they had both gone to live in the north of England. Then the friend decided to return home, leaving him alone. He came to London, he said, because he had nowhere else to go.

'Have you looked for a job?' I asked.

'I – I – I – I – I want to f – f – find a job,' he said, 'b – bb – but I – I – I can't get one that suits me.'

We were within a hundred yards of the Simon Community

and I had to leave. As I watched him go, I wondered if he had ever discussed his problems with the people in charge of the hostels where he stayed. Until now the only people I had seen showing a personal interest in their customers had been the Simon Community.

I sat in a small park in the shadow of a railway bridge, on a seat which caught a few slanting rays of the sun. I heard a rustling noise in the bushes behind me, and I walked round on to the grass. There was a pair of men's legs sticking out from the foliage, squirming. I retreated to a safe distance and watched. The wriggling continued for several seconds, the legs almost disappearing under the bushes; then they reversed out, and a young, clean-shaven man appeared, clutching a bottle. I recognized him as one of my companions from the Night Shelter. He looked around, and strode off down the street.

I walked towards Hampstead Heath. It was a cloudless autumn day, a day when the sun cast bands of warm light across deep cold pools of shade. On Parliament Hill Fields, small boys were carrying giant goal-posts towards soccer pitches marked out on the grass. Their teachers, tall as trees, shouted surnames and pointed, as proud trendy mums looked anxiously from a distance.

I climbed the soft slope to a bench overlooking the field of play. An old man ran down the moist grass, apparently unable to stop. He seemed to be moving in slow motion, his legs bent too far at the knees, so that each step was like a mime artist giving a performance of a man running. At the foot of the slope he slowed down, his legs straightened and he began to walk at normal speed.

I sat on the bench in the sunshine and took out my newly acquired penny-whistle. It was to be my first practice at becoming a busker. I wanted to perfect two sentimental tunes before trying my luck in the subways of central London. I took the advice of a busker I had met a year before. He had told me never to pick a tune that no one knew, and to go straight for the tear-ducts. 'Remember,' he had said, 'you've got about ten seconds to persuade them to put their hands in their pockets, another ten to find a coin, and ten seconds for them to throw the money in your hat.' He had recommended 'Autumn Leaves'. I added a choice of my own, 'As Time Goes By' from the film *Casablanca*.

The combination, I thought, would be devastating.

The notes did not come easily. My fingers felt cold on the bare metal, causing the instrument to squeak like a faulty policeman's whistle. After half an hour I seemed to have lost all feeling in my fingertips and could no longer feel the holes. The notes I was playing seemed to bear less and less resemblance to the tunes I had in mind. I decided to try again the following day.

I walked into Hampstead, skirting the Heath, heading for the nearest branch library to warm myself up. A woman in a tailored coat and velvet gloves opened the door for me as I arrived. She smiled, a smile to cover her embarrassment. I sat at a round table in the centre of the library, where I could view people coming and going to choose their books.

I recognized a dog-trainer I had interviewed a year before. He had invited me to a party only three weeks previously, but he walked past without recognizing me.

I had lunch in a cheap Italian café where the waitress, a young girl who was probably the owner's daughter, seemed frightened to come and serve me. I ordered ravioli and a cup of tea. At the next table, three men wearing the uniforms of London Transport were discussing the aesthetics of tropical fish.

'You're quite right,' said one. 'That great blue dorsal, fucking beautiful, I could sit and look at them for hours.'

One of them looked more serious than the rest.

'Do you remember that bloke who kept a big snake in his fish tank?' he said. 'Remember he put all those bricks across the top to keep it in?'

The others nodded; one of them said he worked in accounts.

'Well, you know he had a budgie as well,' the first man continued. 'He let the bird out in the morning when he went to work, the usual thing, and when he came back the budgie had gone and the snake had lifted all the bricks off the top of the fish tank. All he found were a few feathers.'

The other men roared with laughter. None of them had had much sympathy with people who kept budgerigars anyway. It was difficult to tell if the story had been serious or not. It was cold, and several of the women in Hampstead High Street were wearing furs. I passed a vegetarian café which served tea at a price which was almost double my normal amount, but it looked a warm place to spend a few hours. As I joined the line at the counter, some of the libertarian clientele mistook my rough looks for peasant chic, but then, one by one, they noticed the grime on my shirt, vest and coat. I ordered lemon tea and, ignoring their looks of distaste, took my seat at a long undulating pine table near the window. A plump Irishwoman with cheeks the colour of a spanked bottom was discussing the size of her breasts. Sitting opposite her was a bumptious bearded man whose Dublin accent had almost disappeared, but who played upon the remnants of his origins like a virtuoso of the Uilleann Pipes.

'I don't think you've ever apologized to anyone, except yourself,' said the woman.

'And even that, grudgingly,' he said.

There was a woman with a child at the next table, staring at me. I smiled to myself in the knowledge that the notes I was scribbling on scraps of paper were for the kind of book almost tailor-made for her, the Vegetarian Sociologists of Hampstead. The trouble was that most people like her enjoyed their dirt at one remove, Cartier-Bresson'd, soft-focus, and preferably in the coffee-table version, and here was I rude enough to present it to her neat.

'Do you recognize me?' I asked the man in the fish-and-chip shop where I had been a regular customer for four years.

'Yes,' he said, without remarking on my clothes. 'How've you been keeping?'

My cod roe and chips cost 65 pence, but they only bought me warmth until seven o'clock. Saturday was early-closing day for the café, and I would have to find somewhere else to keep warm until the Night Shelter opened at ten. I walked towards St Pancras Station. In the doorway of a derelict house I saw bright lights. A man with a bright green silk tie was miming to music, surrounded by other men with a video camera, a tape recorder and a monitor screen.

'Who are you?' I asked.

'What it says there,' said a feminine youth with large brown spectacles. He pointed towards a clapperboard which read

'Europien'. He told me they were a band, and they were making their first video.

'We hope to get it shown on West German television,' he said.

The tune seemed monotonous, and the playback was poor quality. They decided to try again.

'What you need for your film,' I said, 'is a tramp to give it a bit of local colour.'

'No thanks,' he said, 'we've already got one,' and he pointed towards the singer.

I had spent £2.55 on food that day, and I realized I would have to economize to keep within my daily budget, even though I still had a free night's accommodation to come. In the buffet at St Pancras Station, I read a discarded newspaper without attempting to buy any food or drink. I switched on my radio at its lowest volume and listened to music. A man with a long beard who looked like a Muslim priest began to sweep the floor around me, and I lifted my feet so that he could pass his brush underneath. Suddenly, I was aware of someone serving me a cup of tea.

'There you go, mate, have that one on me.'

He was young, blond-haired, like a German sailor. He wore a dark jerkin and a fisherman's sweater, and he was already walking away towards a table on the far side of the room. I followed him.

'Who are you?' I asked.

'Never mind who I am,' he said. 'I work on the station here.'

'Well, thanks very much, that's really nice of you.'

He seemed embarrassed. When he left, I asked the woman behind the counter who he was.

'Dunno his name,' she said, 'but he's often in here. I thought it was funny when he asked for two cups of tea.'

I left the station with the feeling that I had not been able to thank my benefactor properly. It was the first spontaneous act of generosity I had experienced in eleven days on the road.

It was bitterly cold when I reached the Night Shelter. The men in the doorway, lacking coats, shivered in spasms which shook their whole bodies. I had been waiting about ten minutes when a woman appeared from the darkness, walking in our direction.

'Oh, fucking hell, look what's coming,' said an Irishman in a fancy knitted cap. 'Bang goes four fucking beds for a kick-off.'

108

We all knew what he meant. If she was staying, she would have to have the entire women's room to herself. She approached me and asked if there were any taxi drivers among us.

'No,' I said, 'this is a hostel.'

'No, no,' she said. 'This is where the taxi drivers are. I was here at 2.30.'

I tried to persuade her she was wrong, but she persisted. Then, after a few minutes, she gave up and walked back the way she had come.

'I knew she was fucking wired-up as soon as she mentioned the taxis,' said the man in the woollen hat.

He stood for a moment, contemplating the hospital across the street. Then he turned to me and said: 'See that building over there? There's thirty dead bodies still in there from that bomb blast or whatever it was, in Soho a few months back. No one's recognized them yet.'

I tried to think back to the events of the past few months, then I remembered. A night-club frequented by South Americans had been deliberately set alight, and dozens of men and women had been killed. I looked at the building across the street. It looked like the outhouse of some farm.

'Do you think they spray them with some chemicals every day to keep the smell down?' said the man in the woollen cap.

'They probably seal them up with something,' said a heavily built Geordie authoritatively.

'Well,' said Woollen Hat, 'you'd soon sober up if you was to fall in there drunk on some dark night.'

I wondered how many of my companions were completely sober that night. None of them looked drunk.

A red-faced young Scot said: 'What a fucking place this is. I've not even had one pint tonight.'

Perhaps that was the point of the Night Shelter, I thought: a kind of social control, a way to stop alcoholics drinking to excess, if only for a few days. Offer them free accommodation, and they would toe the line. The policy seemed to be working.

There was yet another warden on duty that night, a tall man with long hair. The same girl was there, wearing the same shabby black and white clothes.

Woollen Hat looked through the window at the man and said:

'Unpredictable bastard, that one. Sometimes he'll turn you away just for the hell of it.'

There was the usual roll-call, but that night several people were turned away because they smelled of drink. The rest of us made a dash for the kitchen. It was football pools night, and the Mouse Man had been down to King's Cross Station to buy a copy of the following day's *Sunday Telegraph* so that everyone could check their coupons. Racing came first, however, and for the first quarter of an hour I heard little but the tales of complex bets placed that day with the bookmaker. No one mentioned a big win, but they vied with each other for the mathematical ingenuity they claimed to have shown. One man said he had met a mate that day who owed him a fiver.

'He paid me,' he said, 'so I put it all on an accumulator. It didn't do anything, but in any case, he still owes me another fiver.'

An overweight Glaswegian was assigned to the task of reading out the football results, a job he seemed unwilling to take. But seeing that no one else was likely to volunteer, he grudgingly began to announce the scores.

'League Division One,' he said in a broad accent. 'Arsenal two, Sunderland two; Aston Villa three, Tottenham nil.'

'Speak up,' said someone in the far corner.

The Glaswegian cleared his throat and began to shout: 'Coventry nil, Norwich one; Crystal Palace two, Leicester one; Everton two, Liverpool two; Ipswich one, Manchester United one; . . . fucking hell there's a fuck of a lot of draws here,' he said.

He continued through the First Division, pausing several times to comment on the results. Then he stopped and lowered the newspaper.

'What about Division Fucking Two?' said a man at the next table.

'Blackburn one,' he began, 'Chelsea one! Another fucking draw! We've fucking had it this week, lads.'

There were more requests – for the Third Division results and those in the Scottish Divisions, but he had had enough.

'If you want any more,' he said, 'you can read it yoursels.'

He passed the paper to a man on the other side of the table.

110

'Careful with that,' said the Mouse Man. 'I want it to wrap up my clothes.'

The interest in football soon died down. Within ten minutes the conversation was devoted exclusively to racing, and to the contest between Lester Piggott and Willie Carson for the jockeys' championship. I looked for the Trilby, but he was nowhere to be seen.

'I saw him in a caff in Camden Town,' said a man at my table, 'but I have nae seen him since.'

There was no heating in the bedroom when I arrived. The other men were discussing whether or not to ask the warden to switch it on.

'He's a funny bugger,' said Woollen Hat. 'If we ask him, he might not switch it on out of spite.'

'Well, if that's the case,' I said, 'we've lost nothing, because he won't switch it on unless we ask him.'

'I wouldn't be so sure,' said Woollen Hat. 'Best to leave things as they are.'

I went to the warden's office. He was leaning back in a chair, talking to the girl.

'Excuse me,' I said, trying to look as humble as possible.

He turned his head.

'Excuse me, can you switch the heater on in the front room, please?'

'Yeah, sure,' he said, and walked over to a control panel on the wall. I bowed my thanks, staying several seconds longer than I should, to give the impression of looking as vulnerable and suppliant as possible. He did not seem to notice, and resumed his conversation with the girl.

In the morning, there was porridge for breakfast instead of the more usual meal of tea and toast.

'It means they're short of bread,' said the Welshman.

His face looked redder than it had the previous two days.

'I went to the Russell Hotel yesterday,' he told me. 'Fucking bastards. They gave me a job in the laundry room, fucking great rollers, that sort of thing, you know. Told me I'd get twenty quid for two ten-hour days. Then they said they couldn't pay me till the Monday afternoon. Where's the fucking sense in that? I mean, what's the point of working if you don't get cash in hand?

111

So I had the breakfast, good breakfast it was too, and I walked out. I said I'm not coming back on Monday just to collect my pay, so you can fucking stuff it. I mean, it's all right if you've got fifteen pounds in your pocket or something, working on tick, but if you need a fucking sub, what's the point?'

He looked around the room for moral support.

One man said: 'You done right.'

The others looked sympathetic.

The man who had arrived with two black eyes the previous night came in, clean-shaven with the blood cleaned from his nose. For the first time I heard him talk.

'I was mugged,' he said, 'for three fucking quid. I knew one of them as well. He had two mates with him, waiting for me. I couldn't do a fucking thing. They'd waited till I was drunk and I was fucking helpless.'

The way he told the story, it was a natural disaster, like thunder or an earthquake. There seemed to be little rancour in his voice.

'Where are you going today?' the Welshman asked me.

'I dunno,' I said.

'Well, what about the zoo?' he said. 'They're paying eleven pound fifty today, casuals. I'd go myself, only I had this fight with the head waiter there. I haven't been back for six months.'

I asked him what time I should arrive, and he told me nine in the morning.

'There'll be a queue, but they don't care who's at the front and who's at the back. That's what I like about them, no favouritism, see. Not like at Claridge's or some fucking place like that. I've been three times to Claridge's, and never had a fucking sniff. They all buy the supervisor a fucking drink down the pub so he'll take them on the next day. Well, I'm not prepared to do that, see.'

The African was sitting by my bag and my radio and I went over to collect them.

'What are you going to do today?' I said.

'I – I – I – I – I – I'm going to a fffff – ffffriend's,' he said. 'Library isn't open on S – s – s – s – Sundays.'

I looked up and saw five white faces glaring at me. Their expressions had one meaning: traitor. I touched the African on the shoulder.

112

'I'll see you,' I said, and I left the kitchen.

The African stood up almost immediately, wheeling round, his body out of control. At a near-by table a gargoyle-faced man with flowing white hair muttered: 'Look at him, he's in a permanent fucking trance.'

There were seagulls circling above the zoo, jostling for position, waiting to grab the leftovers from feeding time. A group of about fifteen men and one black girl stood inside the back entrance, staring blankly towards the zoo. The standing army of zoo casuals. Some, like me, were first-timers.

'I can't guarantee anything,' said the man at the gatehouse. 'You've just got to take your chance like the rest.'

Many of the others were much smarter than me, wearing clothes which looked almost new. Some of them might have had full-time jobs, I thought, and were just trying to earn a little extra pocket-money on a Sunday. The black girl stood apart, as if she was ashamed to be associated with the rest of us.

'Did you see the wolves?' asked a cockney voice.

'The what?' I said, turning to see a toothless old man in a shabby raincoat.

'The wolves, as you came in. Just round the corner. Vicious-looking bastards.'

'I didn't see them,' I said.

'Did you know Alsatians came originally from wolves?'

'No.'

'Yeah, there was this bloke took his collie dog to Alaska or somewhere like that, and it mated with a wolf in the fucking forest. Yeah. And he took the puppies back with him to Europe. And that's how Alsatian dogs started. Have you ever seen a black Alsatian?'

'Yes,' I said.

'Well,' he said, 'that's the collie in it. And if you ever see a really light-coloured one – you know, fawn or white – that's got more wolf in it than collie.'

We waited for fifteen minutes, then a man in a blazer and red polo-necked sweater appeared by the entrance to a kitchen. He walked like a horse doing dressage, lifting his legs high at the knee.

'Frank, George, Albert,' he said, beckoning three men forward.

The rest of us tried to look eager; I placed my plastic bag in front of me to hide the rips in my coat. It was like being auditioned for a part in the chorus-line. The man in the blazer pranced back to the kitchen.

'Does that thing work?' It was the old man in the raincoat again.

'What?'

'The radio, does it work?'

'Yes,' I said, 'mostly on Radio Two, but it works.'

'This one only cost three pounds ninety-five,' he said, reaching into an inside pocket. He pulled out a plastic radio about the size of a paperback book. It was bright yellow. 'The only trouble with it is, it works for a few minutes, then it clicks off,' he said, switching it on.

There was a loud crackling noise, and he moved a brightly coloured dial to tune it into a station. I could hear the faint sounds of pop music for a few seconds, then nothing.

'I think it's the ampli-flier, myself,' he said. 'A wire's probably got disconnected from the ampli-flier.'

He showed me the back of the radio, where two batteries were held in place by a couple of elastic bands and the back of a packet of Swan Vesta matches.

'It can't be the batteries,' he said. 'They were new a couple of days ago. It must be something like the ampli-flier.'

The curly-headed Irishman who had been sleeping in the flats he was helping to convert was standing just ahead of me in the line. I asked him where he was going to stay that night.

'Don't know, haven't a clue,' he said. He was wearing several sweaters tucked into his trousers, but he had no jacket or coat.

'You're not dressed to stay outside tonight,' I said.

'No, I'll go somewhere like Euston Station and pass the night there.'

A plump woman cook appeared at the kitchen door and called another five people by name. They all walked forward, leaving about seven of us in the line. A tiny black man, whose name had

114

not been called, followed the group, keeping ten paces behind.

'Typical of that lot,' said a white man in a smart anorak, 'they don't know the meaning of a queue.'

Several girls who looked like students passed through the gates and made their way into the zoo, by-passing the kitchen. They were watched every inch of the way by the men. The black girl at the end of our line looked uneasy. Three girls wearing tight jeans arrived together, laughing.

'Look at them, why don't you?' said the Irishman. 'They're fucking gorgeous.' He paused as if he were working out a vital clue in a murder mystery. Then he said: 'I bet they look after the elephants.'

We waited another half an hour before the gatekeeper told us no more casual workers were needed that day. I felt disappointed. I wanted to do something, anything, rather than wander aimlessly about the streets again. I walked into Regent's Park and watched the Sunday footballers limbering up. There was a café on the other side of the changing rooms which seemed to be open, and I went inside. It was run by two school-children, one a boy just about to take his 'O'-levels, the other a girl who was in the sixth form, and who had a career as a chemical engineer all mapped out.

I asked for a cup of tea in my normal, non-dosser's voice. I felt the need to talk to someone on a plane where I did not have to pretend. I asked them how much money they earned for running the café on Sundays, I asked about their schools, and about the jobs they hoped to do. It was such a relief to have a fully stretched mind again, to be speaking in my ordinary voice, that I became almost garrulous. I did not explain who I was or why I was dressed in such ragged clothes, and they did not ask. They gave me a cup of tea and a bread bun.

When I left the café I felt guilty. I had been seeking approval like a child; I had been weak enough to feel the need to step outside my role for no good purpose except my self-esteem. It was beginning to rain, and I was glad. I decided I would walk to the Salvation Army in Blackfriars Road, a distance of some five miles. By the time I reached Great Portland Street the rain was quite heavy. I passed a bronze bust of President Kennedy, whose cheeks were stained with streaks of tarnish like tears. I thought he looked worse than I did in the rain.

A quarter of an hour later, the rain had become so heavy that I was forced to stop in a shop doorway for an hour. It seemed bitterly cold, and I switched on my radio for comfort. There were few people on the streets, and I felt isolated, friendless. A wealthy Chinese woman shared the awning I was sheltering under. She moved as far away as possible, and after a few minutes, she spotted a taxi and flagged it down.

I grew impatient with the rain. How much longer would it pour, I wondered. I began to think I would be trapped under the awning until dark, and I decided to press on. I had walked only a few hundred yards when I was forced to stop again. My hair was soaked, and my coat felt heavy with the water it had absorbed. I waited for the rain to ease a little, then set off once more. I crossed Waterloo Bridge in a rush, dashing towards the shelter of the concrete walkways on the other side. By the time I reached them, my feet were sore. I had felt a blister growing on my left foot, and I sat down on a dry spot of pavement and took off my shoes and socks. The sock, which I had not been able to change for nearly two weeks, had become matted with sweat and had formed a hard ball under my foot. I kneaded it like dough, trying to stretch it back into shape. Passers-by averted their eyes.

I struggled on, limping a little to ease the pressure on my left foot. In Blackfriars Road I passed two men drinking cider in the doorway of an office block. They ignored me. I sheltered under a near-by railway bridge, then I made the final dash to the Salvation Army hostel. The maroon-coloured door was locked, but I could see through a tiny barred hole cut into the door at eye-level. There were men sitting on benches, waiting. One of them saw me and called for the gate to be opened. A small, cheerful Irishman appeared, and he unbolted the door.

'Have you got any beds?' I asked him.

'I'm afraid we've been absolutely full up since Friday night,' he said. 'It's the week-end, you see, and the start of the bad weather. Everyone wants to be indoors.'

I felt devastated.

'Well, where do you suggest I go?' I said.

'Well, you could try Garden Road, you'll find it's free there.

They always have spare beds. Catch a number twelve bus round the corner.'

He shut the gate, and I walked off once more into the rain. At the bus stop, I looked up Garden Road in my street atlas. There were four of them, in different parts of London. I found a phone box, and looked up the Department of Health and Social Security. There was no hostel listed under Garden Road. I wondered if I had misunderstood the Irishman's accent. I looked up Gordon Road. It was even worse: there were twenty-nine of them in my atlas. I decided to cut my losses and walk back to Bruce House, where I felt pretty sure there would be a spare bed. It was two miles away, and by the time I arrived I felt a cold coming on. There was a burning sensation in the back of my throat, and I felt a little feverish.

'You're the third Tony in tonight,' said the man behind the ticket desk.

He seemed cheerful enough, almost welcoming. I began to feel a little better.

In the main television room, hundreds of men were already settled in for the night, many of them with carrier-bags full of bottles. A group of four or five was sharing a bottle of cheap sherry. I sat down at the back, where several old men wore coats as wet as my own. I could smell the distinctive odour of damp cotton and wool. In the far leg of the room two card-schools were in progress, both for sport rather than money. A piggish drunk with a flat nose was tiptoeing from one room to the next, glaring people into a fight. He was almost incapable of standing, and I felt he could have been knocked off balance by the slightest prod of the finger. He stood swaying near the doorway, beckoning to us all. He could find no words to challenge us, but his message was clear: 'Come on, I'll take on any of you.' We all looked steadfastly at the television where an American fantasy detective story was grinding on.

I moved to the next television room, skirting the belligerent drunk, who now seemed to be shouting, yet his lips uttered no sound. A costume drama serial had started; the hero was languishing in jail while his beautiful wife tried desperately to get him released. I sat at the back. The piggish drunk lunged into the room, crashing into a row of chairs. He made his way to a drinking group near the far wall, who included a man with the air of a professor. Perhaps, I thought, he was a member of staff. He told the drunk to sit down and behave himself. Instead, the Pig began to claw at one of the group, demanding a drink. A small man pushed him away several times, but each time he flopped back on to him. The small man then pushed the Pig violently, sending him sprawling into the chairs behind. Both men fell to the floor, fighting. They began wriggling their way under the chairs towards me like a giant insect.

I decided to seek refuge in another room. I made my way once more into the main public room and looked desperately for a safe face, someone I could sit near without starting a fight or risk being embroiled in a drinking party. There were men slumped in their seats with expressions of despair, men trying to understand the infantile plot of the detective story on the screen, men quietly drinking themselves to sleep. A young man began to shout at a sad-faced Pole.

'The Russians are coming to take me away, ha! ha! The Russians are coming to take me away, ha! ha!'

The old Pole swung round and shouted back: 'Am not Russian. Not a Russian, you hear.'

'You're a dirty Polish Jew.'

'Am not a Jew.'

'The Russians are coming to take me away, ha! ha!'

'Not Russian, idiot. Am not Russian, don't you fucking understand?'

The Pole began to curse in his native tongue, a long low curse like a witch casting a spell. The young man laughed.

This taunting depressed me, and I began to feel my fever returning. I looked around the room again and saw an empty chair next to a man in a flat hat who looked clean and in control. Perhaps I could engage him in conversation, I thought. I sat down and saw an old man approach him furtively. He took out a tiny plastic radio. There had obviously been prior dealing.

'This is the one,' said the old man. 'Two quid all right?'

'Yeah, thanks,' said the man in the flat hat.

He opened his coat and took two pound notes from a wallet. The old man handed over the radio with a word of explanation.

'You can only get two channels,' he said. 'The bloke what had it before fixed it so's it'd only play on those two. Look, I'll show you.' He took the back off the radio, exposing transistors and a loudspeaker. He pointed to two components at the top.

'Someone broke the string on the winder, so you'll have to put a new one on. It'll be as good as new then.'

'That's all right,' said the customer, 'I'll soon fix that.'

He examined his new acquisition carefully. I watched with interest as he pulled gently at a wire inside. The wire came loose, away from the solder that had been holding it in place. I thought: he's making things worse. Suddenly, he began to snatch at the wires, pulling them one by one. He grabbed a transistor and yanked it out. He ripped out the aerial, the batteries, the tuning mechanism. He tugged at the loudspeaker, but it seemed too firmly welded on to the front case of the radio. He tried to prise it out with a coin, but still it would not move. He smashed the front of the case with his fingers, pressing against the plastic bars until they snapped. Then he trod on the back until it broke with a loud crack. He tried once more to pull the loudspeaker out, but it would not come loose, so he flung it on the floor, then he calmly fastened his coat and walked away. Beside his chair was a pile of brightly coloured debris. The transistors looked like beads which had broken loose from their string.

I saw the red-faced young Scot who had shivered outside the Night Shelter. I asked him where he had been the night before, since I could not recall seeing him there.

'No, I wasnae there,' he said. 'I got a bit fucking steamed up.'

The fighting drunk was back, still unsteady on his feet but now, apparently, less aggressive. He began a curious dance which involved much shaking of the head and shrugging of the shoulders. It was as if he was apologizing for something, though what it might be I was not sure. His dance visited all parts of the room, where he was universally ignored.

I went to bed early, feeling my fever worsening. My cubicle was on the top floor – the place, according to the Welshman, where all 'the nutters' were billeted. There were three blankets on my bed, and I hoped they would be enough to keep me warm. I found a washroom which had six wash-basins, none with plugs, and several panes missing from the windows. The cold night air made me shiver as I brushed my teeth.

I put my damp coat on the back of the chair in my room,

hoping it would dry by morning. I knew I could not risk it on the bed, feeling as ill as I did. I lay down, hoping for uninterrupted sleep.

At ten past four in the morning I was woken by a loud hammering on the metal door of my cubicle. An Irish voice shouted: 'You're in my fucking bed, get out!'

I sat up. Perhaps I had been dreaming. There was more hammering on the door, very loud hammering. It was no dream.

'Get out of my fucking bed,' said the same Irish voice.

'Fuck off, whoever you are,' I said. 'I've paid for this bed and I'm staying here.'

He hammered on the door again.

'Get out of there, get out. It's my fucking bed. I've got the ticket to this bed.'

My heart was beating very fast. He had woken several men in near-by cubicles. One of them shouted: 'Find another fucking bed, Pat.'

'I've got the ticket to this one,' he shouted.

I got up, and peered over the top of my cubicle by standing on the bed. A broad, tousle-haired Irishman with a black beard stood in the corridor. He looked smaller than me.

'Show me your fucking ticket,' I said aggressively.

He handed me a ticket which showed the number of my cubicle but which was one day out of date.

'This was for last night,' I said.

'Well,' said the Irishman, who seemed to have calmed down, 'at least give me the bag from under the bed, it's mine.'

I found an opaque plastic bag, tied in a knot at the top. Inside, were several heavy objects. I lifted it over the top of the cubicle and gave it to him. Now that he had got what he came for, he became aggressive once more.

'You're still in my fucking bed,' he said.

'Look, I've paid for it and you haven't, so fuck off,' I said.

He walked away, clutching his bag. I lay down and tried to go back to sleep. My heart was pounding. At any minute I expected him to return, and begin the banging on my door once more. There was calm for ten minutes, but I could not sleep. I could hear the other men turning over restlessly too. I waited another ten minutes and my pulse began to settle. I closed my eyes. How much longer, I wondered, before the morning bell rang? The silence continued, and I fell asleep.

CLANG CLANG-CLANG CLANG-CLANG! It was audible several corridors away and much louder than during my previous stay. CLANG CLANK CLANG CLANK CLANG. It was a Monday-morning joke. CLANG-CLANG CLANK CLANG CLANG CLANK CLANG. Whoever was swinging the handbell was clearly enjoying himself. The ringer pushed open the swing door into my section of the corridor. CLANG CLANG CLANG CLANG CLANK CLANG CLANG! He was swinging his arm wildly to create the maximum volume. I could hear him chuckling as he passed. CLANG CLANG CLANK CLANG CLANG CLANK CLANG. When he had gone through our section the man in the next cubicle shouted: 'Fucking bastard!' The bell continued its progress, pausing only for a second as the ringer approached each swing door ahead of him.

I felt very low as I waited in the breakfast queue that morning. My illness heightened my awareness of the desperation around me. In a corner of the dining hall, a wild-haired man wearing a cycling suit under a padded jacket was hitting his own hand, crashing down blows upon himself from a great height. He repeated the blows some fifteen or twenty times, a harsh smacking noise to which no one paid any attention. A man with the profile of Mr Punch stood ahead of me with a cigarette turned dangerously upwards in his lips towards his nose. He looked at this display of violence in a detached way for a few minutes, then he turned to the assembled diners and shouted: 'Seventy-five per cent of the people in this place are loonies – and that includes me!'

It was a morning for staying indoors, a damp cool day that went straight to the chest. But, feverish as I felt, I could not bear the thought of staying in Bruce House a minute longer. I walked past the Theatre Royal where the empty cider bottles and used cans of strong lager were still on the window ledges from the night before. I wandered into Covent Garden, where many of the smarter shops had still not yet opened. I sat outside a delicatessen among a cluster of tables and chairs. My bones felt as though they had been taken out of my body for cleaning and then put back; the back of my throat was now very sore, and I began to wonder what I would do if the virus took a stronger hold. Would it be possible to take to my sick-bed in Bruce House? I doubted it. And what would I do about a doctor? In my identity as Tony Crabbe, no fixed address, I had no doctor, and little chance of getting on to a family doctor's list. In central London, even permanent residents had difficulties, so what chance would I have of receiving a generous reception? If things became worse, I decided, I would go to a hospital casualty department and ask to stay there until I recovered. Yet, at the same time, it seemed to me an extreme measure to have to take for something as simple as influenza, when all I really needed was somewhere warm and comfortable to convalesce.

A waiter at the café-delicatessen was dispatched by the manager to move me on.

'You can't sit here without buying anything,' he said. 'Clear off!'

'What's your name?' I asked him.

'John,' he said.

'Well, I just want to say thank you for that, John.'

I moved to the public benches near by, where two young buskers were tuning up their instruments. There was a straight-backed girl cellist and a pale youth with round wire-framed spectacles who played the guitar. The girl strode her chair like a rider in a hunt and the music soared into the air, her cello cutting great swathes through the morning damp, scattering the pigeons. They had been licensed by the authorities to play there, and both were probably students at a local college of music. As they ran through their rich repertoire of Bach and Cole Porter, the Beatles and Mozart, I thought of my penny-whistle and the two pathetic tunes I had been practising for days now in public parks all over London. I did not seem to be getting any better, and I decided to postpone my busking career, possibly indefinitely.

There was a man selling shirts in the corridor, another selling watches in the dining hall, and a third who had set up a market stall in the television room. Monday night was obviously Market Night at Bruce House.

'What sized collar are you?' said the man pulling one shirt after another out of a large canvas bag like a magician with a top hat.

'Fifteen,' I said.

He searched through his bundle once more, mumbling to himself.

'Sixteen . . . that'll be too big for you. Have you got good eyes? Fourteen, that'll be too small. You did say fifteen, didn't you?'

'Yes, fifteen.'

'Well, how about this one, that looks about your size, try it against yourself. You don't usually wear a tie, do you? It's new, that one, very good value.' It was white, with brown pin-stripes.

'OK,' I said. 'How much is it?'

'That one, well, let's say fifty pence – you'd pay that to put a shirt through the laundry.'

I paid him the money.

'Where do you get them?' I asked, examining the shirt. It had a fleck of paint at the collar, and looked slightly too small.

'I buy 'em, I buy 'em myself,' he said, 'they've all come out the laundry.' He offered no further explanation.

In the corner of the main television room, nearest the door, an Asian had set up two market stalls on the tables. There were baskets of ties, 15 pence each for thin ones, 30 pence for broad ones. Socks were various prices, depending on their condition.

'If they've got holes in, they're cheaper,' said the stallholder.

He sold buttons, needles and thread, razors, shoelaces, toothpaste, toothbrushes, shaving cream, combs, soap – everything a discerning dosser might need. I bought a knitted wool tie for 15 pence, and he thanked me.

In the dining room, an old man was offering watches for sale: cheap shiny timepieces with expanding bracelets and gold-coloured faces. Near by, a younger man was doing good business with tea brewed on a free-enterprise primus stove at 10 pence a cup – 4 pence dearer than the canteen price, but he kept more accommodating hours.

No one objected in principle to black- or white-marketeering; the world of the men's hostel was, curiously, the last place to find socialist feeling. No one I spoke to suggested that society was at fault for their condition. They had grumbles about the way particular parts of their lives were organized, about the stupidity of this or that administrator, but they were all far too wrapped up in their own survival to worry about the system as a whole. There was universal respect for the principle of pulling a fast one, and that was about it.

It seemed to me to be the politics of the prison-house. Many of the people who suffered most were the strongest supporters of the regimes which allowed them the 'freedom' to be drunk, and the 'freedom' to be beaten up. Thus the Salvation Army hostels were the most hated of all because they restricted a person's right to smoke and drink, and they prevented a man with a hangover from lying in. And what were the benefits of clean linen, comparative safety from attack, good food, clean lavatories and orderliness compared with the joy of getting steamed, of mugging and being mugged, of fouling your bed and lying in it too?

The Welshman decided it was time I was initiated into the world of easy money.

'I'll take you to Simpson's in the Strand in the morning,' he said, 'but whatever you do, don't give your real name.'

'Fuck me, no,' said an Irishman sitting with us. 'Tell them anything. I gave the name of the chief cashier of the Bank of England, you know, J. B. Page, the one who signs his name on the pound notes. They never fucking noticed. The only reason they want your name and address is because of the tax. They get a rebate or something for the number of casuals they have.'

'Mind you,' said the Welshman, 'don't go telling any fucker the name you're using. The Social Security have got fucking spies everywhere, man. I mean the fucking bloke next to you in the pub may be one. You know, they buy you a couple of pints and you get talking, and they seem all right, but they're probably from the Social Security.'

He said he and the Irishman had been working a casual shift at the zoo when the Social Security department had a raid.

'And do you know when they did it?' said the Irishman. 'On a fucking Sunday afternoon. They just walked in when all the boys were there, and they nabbed the lot. They looked through the book and found all the names, and half the cunts were signed on under their real names. They did it at Claridge's a couple of months ago. Two blokes came in dressed as kitchen porters. They had them all talking about social security.'

'You can't be too careful,' said the Welshman, 'and you're best off making up a social security number, any fucking thing will do, a car number fucking backwards, anything.'

He told me how to claim free clothes by giving a false name and a false address in Paddington and presenting myself at a day centre in Marylebone, where I would be able to collect a voucher for the WRVS clothes store in Victoria.

'You'll get everything you need there,' he said. 'Fucking new suit, shirt, tie, the fucking lot. I got three pairs of shoes down there, perfect they were, just like fucking new.' His eyes rolled with glee.

He asked me if I had signed on at Scarborough Street. I told him I hadn't, and he gave me detailed instructions about how to claim benefit. It would come to £32.60 a week, he said – about £4 more than I had been allowing myself. I asked him if he had ever considered taking a permanent job.

'At the zoo, they had me three fucking times in the office, wanting me to go regular,' he said. 'I didn't bother, I was earning good money, and I was drawing, that's why I got out of it, before I got fucking lumbered.'

'Oh, it's a dangerous place to work, the zoo,' said the Irishman.

The Welshman said he had been an agricultural worker once, doing casual jobs in the potato and pea fields of Norfolk. He had a reputation, he said, as one of the fastest workers. He had even invented a way of speeding up the gathering of bilberries. He took a comb from his pocket and showed it to me.

'See, you take a tooth out here, and a tooth out there, then you can comb the fucking berries into the sack. None of this fucking one berry at a time, like the rest of them.'

By mid-evening, the drunks who had been shouting and aggressive only half an hour before had either settled into deep sleep over the dining-room tables or were leaning hard back in their chairs, snoring. The Welshman thought the time was ripe to sell me his meal voucher for cash. I paid him £1 for a voucher worth £1.10.

'I could use the cash to buy some fags,' he said. 'I'll give you my bed ticket to go with it, so the two match up.'

In the main television room a television serial based on Victor Hugo's *Les Misérables* had just begun. It was a loud American production, and it woke some of the drunks up. A man lurched past me, attracted by the sound.

'He's the better for drink,' said a ginger-headed Irishman to my right.

The manager of the hostel, a tall man who looked like a petty clerk, followed the drunk in. He stood for a second, looking around, then he spotted a man two rows ahead who was drinking from a can of lager. He virtually ran towards him, and grabbed the can.

'Right,' he said, 'you, out.'

He marched the man out of the room as an example to the rest. I felt sorry for him – he had been one of the quietest drunks in the room, while the men in the centre of the room with alcohol roaring round their brains grinned inanely at each other, congratulating themselves on their luck. They had had the foresight to get drunk either off the premises or out of sight. It seemed to me the most token regulation by the hostel staff; if drunkenness were the offence, I thought, why not throw out the drunks; and if drinking alcohol on the premises were the offence, why make such infrequent checks? One of the men in the centre started pushing another around, and I felt I had to leave.

I hurried through the turnstiles, and turned left, past the Theatre Royal and round the corner. There was a pub, a small old-fashioned place with bowed windows heavily engraved. It looked warm and comfortable, too good for someone dressed as I was, but I decided to risk rebuff.

Surprisingly, the barmaid welcomed me, and even apologized for the price of her beer. I sat down on a side of the pub that was empty, and watched three sinuous girls and a shy Malaysian youth walk in. They looked like dancers.

The girl in thigh-length boots and very tight jeans said: 'Have you had to undress altogether?'

'Not yet,' said her skinny friend.

The third girl said: 'Your skin has to be so bloody perfect. Even water can bring me out in a rash.'

I tried to concentrate on my beer.

Groups of theatre-goers began to crowd the pub; some declaimed, others listened. I could understand why many people were deterred from going to the theatre. I sat in the corner and watched, like a man at his own funeral, itching to be rude, but forbidden to join in the conversation.

It was 10.45 when I returned to Bruce House – I had delayed my return as long as possible to give myself the opportunity of investigating the other fire escape. I wanted to find out if that, too, had padlocked doors.

I climbed the stairs to the fifth floor. Several inmates had wedged chairs under their doors, presumably because the bolts on the other side were not working. I wondered how quickly they would be able to move them if a fire broke out, especially if they were drunk. There was urine in the corridors as usual, and at the head of the secondary fire escape the smell was overpowering. This was obviously the place favoured by those people too drunk to find the well-hidden lavatories on the same floor. I stepped carefully down the stone staircase until I reached the fire doors at the bottom. To my dismay, they were padlocked too. There was the same notice as before, advising residents to notify the front office before opening the doors. There was also a container for a key, advising inmates to break the glass in case of fire. But there was no key.

As I returned to my bed, I could hear men striking matches in their cubicles. Smoking was forbidden, but there seemed no attempt to enforce the rule. I examined the mattress on my bed when I reached my own cubicle. It was made of plastic foam, a substance which gave off toxic fumes when set alight. To my horror, I saw that there was a burnt patch the size of a dinner plate on the underside – the sleepers on my floor had had a lucky escape the last time.

Violence came early the following morning. It started well before eight o'clock in the corridor about twenty yards from where I was getting dressed. A muscular white youth with tattoos on his arms was threatening to kill one of the porters, a black African who wore a neat grey suit. The porter had received a complaint that the youth was in the wrong bed, and he had asked him to move his belongings.

'I've done fucking time for cunts like you,' said the tattooed youth, grabbing the porter by the lapels, 'and I'll do it again if I have to.'

Two shift workers further up the corridor joined in the argument, taking the side of the white youth.

'Shut up, you black bastard,' said one, 'you're like an old woman. Let's get some fucking sleep down here, or I'll come and sort you out myself.'

I did not envy the porter his job.

I found it curious that such an aggressively male society should tolerate homosexuality so openly. At breakfast, a down-at-heel dizzy blond posed and pouted as his ageing hippie lover caressed him in public view. It was a desperate relationship, founded more on display than affection. The blond, a youth in his late teens, was clearly in control. He was a grubby slice of cheesecake who fluttered his eyelashes at anyone who passed. He kissed his lover passionately on the lips, then turned to make sure everyone was watching.

'He wants his fucking arse kicking,' said the Welshman, watching me eat.

I had used his meal voucher to buy myself some breakfast – sausage, and a mixture of instant mashed potato and processed peas. It had used up only 45 pence of the voucher, and I found I could not even finish it. The Welshman seized his opportunity.

'Aren't you going to eat that?' he said.

'No, I can't face any more,' I said.

He took my plate, and spread the mashed-potato mixture like butter on to a slice of bread. Then he folded it over and began to eat.

'No sense in wasting, is there?' he said. 'Can't see what you're eating this way.'

We walked to the Strand, and just before we reached the entrance to Simpson's restaurant, we turned down an alleyway which led to an entrance marked 'Staff'. The Welshman led the way. Through the door, we seemed to be on a cat-walk, a metal fire escape that descended to the bowels of the building. There was a timekeeper's office on a platform, and the Welshman spoke to a man behind the glass.

'Any casuals going today?' he said.

'No,' he said, 'not at the moment.' He looked at me and asked me if I had been there a couple of days before.

I thought for a moment, wondering if my answer could get me into trouble.

'No,' I said.

'Oh, sorry,' said the timekeeper.

When we were outside again, the Welshman said: 'You fucking idiot, he was going to give you a fucking job. You should have said yes.'

We parted company, he in search of more free soup and bread, I in search of work. I decided to play things straight, and go to a Job Centre. It was in Kentish Town, a bright friendly place that looked like a travel agents' office.

'Job preference?' said the application form.

'Anything,' I wrote.

'District preferred?'

'Anywhere.'

'Are you prepared to work any hours?' said the form.

'Yes,' I replied.

The matronly woman adviser crossed out my minimum earnings requirement of £33 a week.

'I think we can do better for you than that,' she said.

She told me to report to the Unemployment Benefit Office up the street.

It was much more institutional: a large, bare, gloss-painted room with about thirty people waiting to be called. Three girls who had just left school were determined to make a joke of everything that happened.

'Mr Johnson,' called one of the officials on the other side of the counter.

'Mr Johnson,' mimicked one of the girls.

The man made his way to the front of the room. He was blushing.

'Were you truly wafted here from Paradise?' said the girl to her friend, imitating the voice of an actor in an advertisement.

'No, Luton Airport,' said her friend.

They both laughed.

I felt angry. It seemed to me they were degrading the people who had come to claim benefit – the anxious dumpy woman who walked round the back of everyone to avoid the stares, the nervous young teacher twiddling his lighter, the man with the permanent lop-sided grin. For all of them, signing on was not a joke, not something you could mock.

After an hour and a quarter, I was called for my interview. A pretty, nervous girl gave me a form – B1 – which she told me to take to the Social Security Office at Scarborough Street. She said I would be able to claim benefit there, and that I should return to the Unemployment Office on Thursday. It had all been very civilized – so far.

The Scarborough Street office, set aside for claimants with no fixed address, had closed for that day. In any case, it would have been a two-hour walk to get there, and I was glad I would be spared that trauma for a while. But there was another trauma to come – the Spike.

I had thought that the Camberwell Reception Centre would be just another place to stay, a hostel like all the others. I did not bargain on the Workhouse. It was a massive Victorian fortress built more than a century before, a fortress that had become the dark satanic repository for the twentieth-century poor. It was a prison designed to keep people out rather than in, a place where no one should ever want to return.

I arrived just before eight in the evening, a traveller looking for a place to stay.

'How much money have you got?' said a gross, aggressive man in a crew-necked sweater.

'Four pound,' I said. It was all the money I had on me.

'Count it out, will you?' he said.

He made me read a notice which said that every person admitted to the centre must be bathed on admission, and that, if so required, must give up his clothes to be dry-cleaned. I did not have time to read any more when a tall well-dressed man took me to one side.

'Who sent you here?' he said.

'Who sent me here? Well . . . nobody.'

'Book into a hostel. Carrington House. Get a 36 bus for Deptford.'

'Can't I stay here?'

'No, you've got money, no. Just get on a bus . . .'

'You don't seem very sympathetic . . .'

'No, I'm not really, no.'

'Why not?'

'Because you've got money. You can book in there.'

I was out on the street again, rejected by the Camberwell Reception Centre because my £4 made me too rich to stay. I did not understand why. No one had explained. Nor did I know where to catch a No. 36 bus. I made my way back into the city centre. The bus fare cost nearly 60 pence. There was another government reception centre in Soho, called West End House, and I tried my luck there. The bright metal doors were locked.

'We're full up,' said a voice from inside.

'Well, where do I go?' I said.

'Try Centrepoint down the road.'

The only Centrepoint I knew was the famous office block at the end of Oxford Street. I spent half an hour looking for a hostel near by with no success. It was 9.30 and I still had not eaten. I bought myself a meal and a drink. My money was now down to less than a pound.

I found Centrepoint by accident. It was a hostel for the young and vulnerable near Piccadilly Circus, and I was refused entry once more.

'I'm afraid you're really too old for us,' said the girl at the entrance. 'You could always try Camberwell, they've always got beds.'

'But I've just come from there,' I said.

'Why wouldn't they take you?' she asked.

'They said I'd got too much money at the time,' I said.

'Well, if you like, what I can do is phone up and see if they're sending a bus to Charing Cross tonight, and they'll be able to give you a lift back down there. OK?'

She disappeared into the hostel, and returned five minutes later with the news that I was now poor enough to stay.

'What they said was that if what you're saying is really on the line and straight, then there's no reason why they can't review your case, starting again.'

The van arrived at midnight. It was a dark green mini-bus with enough room for about twelve people in the back. The driver was accompanied by an academic-looking middle-aged man and a fair-haired girl who looked like a student. They seemed like observers rather than helpers, asking the driver question after question.

In the back of the bus, a wild-haired Irishman, dark like a Flamenco dancer, climbed in opposite me. He told me he had once been a waiter in Blackpool, but had been forced to give up the life because he met a girl.

'It wasn't her fucking fault, really,' he said. 'I mean, I should never have married her. But it seemed like a good idea at the time. I had my hands tattooed with her name and all, you know, on both fucking hands. Well, I'd never have got another job as a waiter after that, not with those tattoos, so I had to give it up.'

He offered me a sip of tea, but I declined politely. Did I want a drag on his cigarette? No, thanks all the same.

The van set off with a jerk, careering towards Holborn. There were five of us in the back, and we had to told on tight to the seats to stop ourselves hitting the sides. In the front, separated by a transparent plastic screen, the blonde girl continued with her questions, but I could hear none of the words.

At Lincoln's Inn Fields, the van turned sharply into the park and stopped by a bandstand. A shadowy figure appeared from the darkness, blinking in the headlights.

'Peter,' said the Irish waiter. 'Come in, Peter, we'll get you a bed for the night.'

The man hesitated for a few seconds, then he peered in the back of the van.

'Fuck me,' he said, 'it's you. I was expecting the soup van.'

'Come in, come in,' said the Waiter. A painfully thin man, wearing a crumpled outsized suit, clambered aboard. His face was badly bruised.

'I was going to sleep in the bandstand,' he said, 'but it's great to see you. Where have you been?'

'Oh, I've been doing a fair old stretch,' said the Waiter. 'I've been away for quite a time.'

The van set off again, speeding towards Waterloo, tilting hard at every corner. The driver seemed to be showing off to the blonde girl.

'And how have you been since you got out?' said the thin man. 'Have you been well?'

'I've been taking a good few hidings from the police,' said the Waiter. 'Not that I haven't given a few back. But they're wicked bastards all the same. They said they were going to fit me up for something, just to get me out of the way. That's why I won't sleep rough at the moment – too much risk of being picked up.'

We stopped at Waterloo Station, down an alley off the forecourt. A group of wraiths were warming themselves by a brazier. Dickens's London, I thought. The driver opened the back doors of the van and invited the ragged men inside. A pale-faced wretch started to move forward, then someone shouted: 'Don't get in there, it's the fucking Spike van.' He stopped abruptly and walked back to the others. The driver shut the door and checked the tyres, then we were on our way again, plunging into the darkness of South London.

The Waiter said: 'They've done for my brother – do you remember him, Peter? I went to see him a couple of months ago. That last hiding finished him, he's a fucking vegetable.'

The two men talked about Bruce House, and the Waiter was interested to know whether the young homosexual was still there.

'She's a bold queen, fuck me, she is,' he said.

He asked me if I had ever been in the Spike. I told him I had not.

'Well,' he said, 'just remember to hang on to your clothes. I had my fucking socks pinched the last time I was there. They're like animals in that place.'

The journey lasted about twenty minutes, and by the time the van pulled into the Spike yard, I felt badly shaken. The driver told us to report to the entrance house, and as we filed across the yard, I saw the professor and the blonde girl observing us, asking questions of one of the officials as we passed by. The official pointed at me.

'The one with the radio,' he said.

I gave my name and age to the man at the reception desk. Like the first man, earlier in the evening, he could not spell my first name – Tony.

'Is that T – o – n – i?' he said.

He asked me to read the notice listing all the rules of the reception centre. The notice said that I had to obey all reasonable orders. Why orders, I wondered. Was I not still a civilian?

'Come on,' shouted a young black man dressed in casual clothes. 'Shower!'

He pointed towards the door at the end of the corridor. I moved aside to let someone pass.

'Come on!' he shouted again.

He hurried me into a drill-hall of a room which had changing cubicles at one end and a huge battery of showers at the other. There seemed to be about thirty of them, their plumbing arching over like the street lights down the central reservation of a motorway. I could see the heads of several men washing themselves.

'Take off your top and bring me your clothes,' said a man who looked like a gym instructor.

As I undressed, I could hear the staff in the corridor shouting names and numbers. It sounded like an army camp – or a prison. The gym instructor searched my vest for lice, then, satisfied that my clothes were free of vermin, told me to have a shower.

The shower was warm, and I began to relax under the jets of water. It was my first full wash since I had taken to the road two weeks before and I intended to make the most of it. The heat seemed to make the aching in my bones ease a little, but the water also made my nose begin to stream. I heard a man shouting something like my fictional name.

'Crabby, Craby?' he said, walking along the line of showers, looking in each tiled cubicle in turn. He stopped at my shower, like a sergeant inspecting a new recruit.

'Craby?' he said.

'It's Crabbe,' I answered.

'Have you got any means of identification?' he said. He looked down at my naked body. I felt tempted to search for imaginary pockets.

'No, nothing,' I said. 'I've got a ticket for Bruce House in my coat.'

'Has it got your name on it?'

'Yeah . . . I mean, no, but you can ring them up and check.'

I wondered what they were trying to find out. None of the others had been asked for means of identification. In any case, this was not a bank or a top security establishment – there seemed nothing worth stealing. He took the ticket from my coat and walked away. A few minutes later, he returned, and the interrogation continued.

'Did you come here earlier today?' he asked.

I told him I had been refused entry because I had too much money.

'So you've still got money,' he said.

'No.'

'So where is it?'

'I've spent it on food. I've had a meal tonight.'

'Spend it on booze?'

'I've had a couple of pints, yeah.'

He returned my ticket and walked away again. I continued to shower, washing my matted hair with soap. To my horror, the water round my feet began to turn dark red. The powder which had been put in my hair by the BBC make-up department to simulate dirt contained a soluble dye. It looked as though I was bleeding, great streaks of red ran down my body, forming a dark pool at my feet. I looked over the top of the cubicle. The men who had been showering further down the room had abandoned their towels on the side, and had now dressed and gone. I decided to dry my hair, and then substitute my stained towel for one that they had left. I could not risk any more suspicion falling on me, and that dye was very suspicious indeed. I waited for my moment, then I made the switch.

As I dressed, I thought how absurd my cloak-and-dagger activity had been, and yet I had been treated as a threat from the start, as an intruder into their world. I felt I had taken the Queen's shilling, and forfeited the right to be treated as an ordinary citizen.

We were told to wait in the next room for interview. I joined the others on a series of plastic bench seats. I felt like a patient waiting for treatment. In front of us were a row of open cubicles, where interviewers sat behind desks, filling in the answers to the questions they were asking.

'Why are you asking all these questions?' said the man facing an African-born official.

'Well, let's put it this way,' said the official. 'There are eight hundred people staying here tonight, and if there was a fire, we'd need to account for everyone. You might be killed and we wouldn't know who you were. Anything could happen to you during the night.'

It was hardly the most comforting of explanations.

It was my turn. The African beckoned me forward. He asked me my age, height, date and place of birth. Under a section labelled 'build' he wrote 'broad'.

'Religion?'

'I haven't got one,' I said.

'Were you a Christian at all when you were born?' he asked.

'Well, I suppose so,' I said. 'Me mum and dad were, yeah.'

'Er . . . Church of England then.'

'But I'm not Church of England . . .'

He had already written it down. 'Next of kin?'

He asked me again why I had been refused admission earlier.

'You had too much money?' he said. 'How many thousands have you got?'

I told him I had had £4 and I now had 54 pence.

'Well, I suppose we'll have to let you in,' he said.

'I don't know what all this stuff is about the money,' I said, ''cos I were quite willing to pay earlier. I didn't understand. Nobody explained what were sort of going on.'

He said: 'There must have been something more than that. Still, not to worry. Sign there.'

I asked him why he had asked me so many questions, and what he was going to do with the information.

'It doesn't matter,' he said. 'It's for our own information. We just want to know how many people we've got in the centre, who they are, what is their name, if there's anything happens to them who to contact and so forth. Just to keep a record of how many people we have in the centre, that's all. We're not giving it to the Gestapo or something.'

He told me to report to another cubicle round the corner. A

bored man was lounging in a chair. He handed me a ticket.

'Block N's straight across the yard,' he said.

I studied the ticket. I was in Block N, Floor 2, bed No. 13.

'You collect your blankets through the door, down the corridor on the left,' he said.

In the yard it was pitch dark. One o'clock in the morning. I could make out the shapes of what looked like two massive black warehouses, great cliffs against the night sky. There were lights over to my right, in a smaller building, and I walked carefully across, looking for the letter 'N'. The lights came from a huge washroom, a beacon of fluorescent light which made the other buildings seem even darker. There was no one inside, and I wandered towards the warehouses. I could make out fire escapes and dark windows, but little else. There were outbuildings which formed dark alleyways, and I dared not walk down them without being able to see my way out. I wondered where the others had gone. A shadowy figure appeared at the end of the second warehouse. I could not make out his face, but his voice sounded like the Irishman called Peter we had picked up from the bandstand at Lincoln's Inn Fields.

'I'm looking for Block N,' he said.

'So am I,' I said.

We peered at the nearest building to see if there was a sign painted on the brickwork. It was too dark to see. We followed the fire escapes, black exoskeletons clinging to the massive sides, but the alley was blind. There were several flights of steps leading to gloomy doorways, but each door we tried was locked. We went to the centre of what seemed to be a connecting building between the two warehouses. There was an open door, and a dim light inside, but we could still see no letter 'N'.

'This must be it,' said Peter, the Irishman. He pointed to a blurred outline on one of the bricks by the door.

'It looks like an "N", then again it could be a "G",' he said.

It looked to me like a crack in the brick itself. We opened the door and entered a broad gloss-painted corridor. I could smell disinfectant. Opposite us was a sign which read 'Sick Bay'.

Peter looked hard at it and said: 'Six bay . . . er . . . sick bay.'

We followed the light to the end of the corridor where a nervous young man in a white coat sat behind a broad counter framed by a large hatch. There was a strong smell of disinfectant here which seemed to be coming from the piles of blankets behind him.

'Is this Block N?' I asked.

'Yes, do you want blankets?'

He looked strangely guilty. He gave us three blankets each, and we carried them up to the second floor.

There was a tall double door with a padlock hanging from one of the catches, and grubby finger marks all around the lock. Inside was a long room containing about 150 beds. I looked for numbers painted on the frames of the double bunks, but it was too dark to see. There were four red lights on stalks, like torches, near the ceiling, shedding an eerie, blood-coloured light on the bodies below. I walked backwards and forwards, looking for a number, any number.

'Just go anywhere,' said a voice from one of the bottom bunks.

I followed his advice, and began to put my blankets on a top bunk near the centre of the room. The mattress was covered in plastic, like those used in hospitals for incontinent patients. I used one of my blankets to cover it, then laid the other two on top. I decided not to undress too far, in case the Waiter had been right about the other men stealing my clothes. I wrapped my radio in my overcoat and used it as a pillow. The rest of my clothes I stuffed inside my plastic bag, and hung it on the bed-post near my head. I hoped that the rustling of the plastic would wake me before anyone had a chance to steal anything.

The blankets felt surprisingly smooth; I had expected them to scratch my skin. As I lay there, several men passed by, stealing sly glances from one side to the other; on the prowl. The thin Irishman was joined by the Waiter, and they began to bandy prison experiences and stories of crimes they had committed. It was clear that the thin man was in a much lower league of villainy, mostly petty theft. He asked his friend about an armed robbery he had been involved in.

'Were you sober for that job?' he said.

'As a fucking judge,' said the Waiter.

'What did they ask you downstairs?' said the thin man.

'Oh, the usual. The Grand Inquisition. He asked me how much money I'd had at the beginning of the day, so I told him

– eighteen quid. Well, your man says he's fucking amazed how honest I am, you know? He says what did I spend it on, so I told him I gave fourteen quid to a mate to repay a debt, and I bought a few jars with the rest. Well, says he, aren't you ashamed to come here? Why should I be ashamed, I tell him. Without people like me, I said, you'd have no fucking customers at all.'

I tried to sleep, but the Waiter continued to talk for more than an hour: stories of fights with the police, of the inhospitality of the English. The man in the bottom bunk to my left began to masturbate, his entire bunk swaying to and fro. There were two cross-members missing from the top of his bunk, and the bed-frame began to gyrate like a hula-hoop dancer. A man across the room began to talk in his sleep.

'Take any bed,' he said. 'This is my daughter, take any bed.'

Three hours later, I was woken by a blinding light. A deep voice bellowed: 'All right now, early risers!'

Five o'clock. Who, I wondered, would be getting up at this time? Two men dressed and left, but the lights were left on, lights which seeped under my eyelids as I tossed this way and that. It was another hour before I fought my way back to sleep again. At 7.30, I heard a gong in the yard outside. The thin Irishman stretched himself long and hard.

'That was the best night's sleep I've had in six months,' he said.

I folded my blankets and carried them downstairs. I felt ill once more, aching and feverish. The man at the hatch told me to go into a back room, where a group of men were stacking blankets into racks. They looked like trusties rather than staff. There were men everywhere doing chores, sweeping here, cleaning there. I wondered what my own chore would be.

In the corridor a man on crutches wearing a dirty trenchcoat hobbled in front of me, singing a verse of 'The Old Rugged Cross' at the top of his voice. The hollow men in the breakfast queue shuffled forward into the grey light, lining up five deep on the fire escape outside.

'Why don't you young fellas join the army?' said the man in the trenchcoat. 'Do yourselves some good. Living this life. Christ, they wouldn't have you at that!'

The others seemed to have heard the speech many times

before. The old soldier's face had the ruddy complexion of the alcoholic, the kind of colouring which could be mistaken for good health.

'Don't even call it an army now,' he said. 'What, killing kids. Blowing up women and children. Fucking cowards, aren't they? Catch 'em on their own, boy . . .'

A young bearded man with sunken cheeks approached me and seemed to start making a serious speech. He made his points with conviction, speaking forcibly and at length. But none of his words made proper sentences, and I could gather no sense at all.

We entered a large hall which seemed to have been a chapel at some stage in its history. It had large gothic windows in the end wall, and there were tables laid end to end to make long institutional boards, the knives, forks and spoons already laid. A man with a large ladle was spooning cornflakes into dishes, handing them to another man who poured warm milk on top. Once more I was reminded of Dickens. The staff remained severe and aloof, and a young man directed us to our seats like a schoolteacher, filling first one table, then the next.

'Next table,' he told me, unsmiling.

I passed a cluster of mugs on the end of the table, each brimming with tea, but my hands were already full with my radio, my bag and my cornflakes. By the time I sat down at the far end of the table my passage back was blocked. In front of me were slices of bread and a bowl of butter. Further up the table was a bowl of marmalade, but by now it had started its journey to the far end. I watched as the last of it was scooped from the bottom of the dish. The warm milk had made the cornflakes coagulate and I could eat only a few mouthfuls. I pushed the bowl to one side, causing the others to look on in amazement. This was not the behaviour of a survivor. The next course was a dog bowl full of Italian tomatoes and a slice of bacon.

'Do you want mine?' asked the dignified old man to my left.

'Yes, please,' I said, and I tipped the contents of his bowl into my own, mopping up the tomatoes with my bread.

'Did you know,' said my neighbour, 'a world revolution started in the Britannia public house? A world revolution all over the world. It's what they call an Allah revolution. They're like children, about that big, and they get children. And they don't

140

need a drink or smoke. Little children, you see. Everyone was caught unawares.'

'And it started in what pub?' I said.

'The Britannia public house. Rule Britannia . . . little children that big. If you come from out in the country, you don't know what's been happening, do you?'

The man opposite said he was due for a medical that morning, and he was worried that the doctors might find something wrong. Suddenly a voice boomed from a loudspeaker.

'Greaves, Bernard, Rogers, Ruddles, Gilmore, Roberts . . .'

The man on the other side of the table held his breath until he heard his name, then he relaxed. There was nothing he could do about it now, he was down on the list.

'He'll call you in a minute,' he told me.

'Why?' I asked.

'For the Welfare.'

'What's that?'

'The Welfare woman. All the first-timers have to see her.'

The loudspeaker boomed again. This time it was the call for the Welfare. My name was last, and they had got it wrong again. 'T. Crabtree,' said the announcer. 'Come out if your name's been called.'

There were sixteen of us in all, and we were sent to the interview room where I had been asked questions by the African the night before. Few of the others seemed to be first-timers; several looked like permanent residents.

An old man who wore a leather glove because of some skin complaint went through a litany of fantasies which the others seemed to have heard before.

'I've got fifty thousand pounds whenever I need it,' he said. 'And that's my red Rover car, I got it straight off the production line at Ford's.'

A group of three boys who looked no older than eighteen began to taunt the old man, forcing him to change seats. Then two of them began to mock their friend, an effeminate youth who looked as though he had dyed his hair black and was wearing mascara.

'Isn't she lovely?' said one of the boys, and he began to whistle at his friend as though he were calling a dog.

141

'Stop it,' said the boy with the mascara.

I watched as the speechmaker I had seen in the breakfast queue walked up and down, scoring unintelligible debating points off himself. The soles of his shoes were connected to the uppers only at the toes, so that I could see his bare heels as he walked.

The Welfare Lady was late. A voice from somewhere in the next room shouted that there had been a hold-up at the post office, but she would soon be on her way. Then a man in a white coat appeared. He had a kindly face, and offered to get the old man with the gloved hand some new underwear. A man with a nervous twitch at the back said he would like some new underpants as well.

'All right, I'll get you some,' said the man in the white coat.

He returned a few minutes later, carrying dark-blue underwear for both men, but the man with the twitch had disappeared.

'He didn't say where he was going,' said the man who had been sitting next to him.

White Coat went to the door of the yard and called a man over.

'Here,' he said, 'stuff these in your pocket,' he said, handing the man the underwear.

There were several inmates sweeping the yard. A man with a broom stood by the waste-bins and shouted, 'Plenty of spare food for them as wants it.' He lifted the lid of the bin. There was another message from the far room about the progress of the Welfare Lady.

'She's arrived, and she's sorting out the money. Shouldn't be long now.'

She was in her early thirties and pretty. She took me and two other men to her office at the front of the building. While the first man went in for interview, I talked with the other in the corridor outside. He was in his fifties, from Southampton, and he told me he had a record as an 'unreliable worker'. He hated the Spike, he said, but found it addictive.

'It gets to be a habit,' he said. 'You'd be surprised, you let yourself do it all too easily, it's like a merry-go-round, once you get on it. It's all right getting on, but it's hard to get off.'

He said he only knew of the Camberwell Spike by repute.

'This is a hole in the bottom of the world,' he said. 'This is the lowest of the lot, and the roughest of the lot.'

I said I did not understand why the officials there did their best to deter people from staying.

'You can't come in a place like this expecting common sense,' he said, 'because half the people who come here are potty. Whatever the rules are, you obey them, and that's it. They never do make any sense.'

My interview with the Welfare Lady lasted about a quarter of an hour. She asked me if I had a prison record, if I was an alcoholic or a drug addict, and if I had served in the armed forces.

She said since I had not found work, I should think about returning home to Doncaster to live with my mother, or persuade a friend to let me stay on his floor. It was the only way I would find proper work, she said.

'It's a vicious circle, isn't it? An employer doesn't like someone with an unsettled way of life. Say you wanted a job in a bank or somewhere like that, well, you just haven't got a proper address to give anybody, have you? I mean, the only sort of jobs you're going to get are casual jobs.'

I wondered why she thought I was a potential employee in a bank, but she found my appearance less shocking than most. My clothes she pronounced 'not bad actually' and 'adequate', and she said I had done 'pretty well so far'. She said I needed somewhere permanent to 'make myself presentable for interviews', and she advised me to claim Supplementary Benefit.

It was good advice, but it was a direct contradiction of the official government policy of the time. The politicians had decided that people like Tony Crabbe should be prepared to move to where the jobs were, and that meant the London area and not the north, where she had advised me to return. She told me never to return to the Spike.

'Men we take on for residence are men who are unable to support themselves, either physically or mentally,' she said, 'because they've got a drink problem, because they're mentally unable to cope. I don't think you are.'

*

It was mid-morning before I took my usual seat in St Pancras Library. It was a cold day outside, and the library seemed unusually warm. I became aware of my own smell more than usual, a phenomenon I found ironic in view of my first shower less than twelve hours before. Perhaps, I thought at first, I was more aware of the smell of my clothes because I was comparatively clean. But it was not mere imagination. The student on my left gathered her books and left hastily, the one on the right stuck it out until she had finished the page she was writing. She put the cap on her pen and glared at me. I almost offered to leave, but she motioned me to stay where I was; she did not want to inflict me on others.

I slept for two hours, pretending to read a copy of *The Economist*.

I resolved to change my ways. It seemed perverse to continue my progress towards dereliction, when most of my fellow dossers kept up appearances of a kind, and when most of them did casual work. Even the men who slept under Charing Cross Arches had talked about casual jobs. From then on, I decided to try all the ways I could think of to clean myself up and find work. But first, I had an appointment at Scarborough Street.

The Supplementary Benefit Office at Scarborough Street, East London, looked like a small modern factory anywhere: a block of dreary bricks from an architect's pattern-book, anonymous, featureless. But inside, on benefit days, it was a gaudy vision of Hell, a Hieronymous Bosch painting of souls in torment, courtesy of the Welfare State.

I arrived at about 11.30, two hours after the first sherry bottles had been broached. Many of the claimants had already formed themselves into drinking parties, a quiet gentlemanly affair at the front involving a bottle of 'Old England', a sharp vicious affair at the back involving the bad end of a bottle of 'VP'. The staff kept well out of harm's way behind toughened glass screens on the perimeter of the room.

I joined the queue near the door, clutching the B1 form I had been given at the unemployment office. I knew from the start that I did not qualify for benefit, because the man whose role I was playing did not exist. But I was curious about Scarborough Street. I wanted to know what it felt like to join the other dossers in the place where they spent so many of their idle hours.

I was curious, too, to find out if the tales I had been told of a vicious and abusive staff were true. Was it credible that officials of the Welfare State would delight in delay, savouring the power they held over the unfortunate casualties of society? I had heard numerous such tales, stories of injustice, of benefit denied, because some petty official took exception to a face. And as for entitlements that went by default, it was, in my circle of friends, common knowledge that 'discretionary' meant 'unobtainable'.

I was tenth in the queue. Ahead of me, I could see a notice telling me I must have means of identification – a passport, a tax form or a similar document. Because I was not Tony Crabbe, I had none. The notice mentioned hostel receipts as though no one who went to Scarborough Street would possibly live elsewhere. Ahead of me stood a skeleton of a man in an outsized check jacket, like a clown's. He was clutching a Habitat catalogue. Did he live in a hostel, I wondered. Two shaven-headed youths began to taunt him.

'You're a fairy,' said one, and then whistled, the same whistle I had heard in the Spike, like a man calling a dog.

The skeleton turned on the youths.

'You're nothing but dirty perverts,' he said.

He turned, huffily clutching his catalogue tighter. Then he turned again to face the shaven-heads.

'And you wear make-up, you perverts,' he said.

He looked again towards the front. One of the shaven-heads crept forward and touched him on the shoulder, causing him to wheel round in alarm.

'Come on, come on, fight, you cowards,' said the old man, scuttling out of reach. 'You daren't fight, you perverts.'

He danced as he shouted, bobbing up and down on his toes like a ballerina. It was what everyone had been hoping for. He was the regular floor-show at Scarborough Street.

I hated the shaven-heads for their cruelty, more especially because one of them seemed to be provoking the old man for the entertainment of his girl friend. She was a Pre-Raphaelite girl whose face was quite beautiful in repose, but she had an ugly laugh, a laugh big enough to hide behind.

It was my turn at the head of the queue. The civil servant behind the screen was young and casually dressed. In the street I might have mistaken him for a student. His expression was pugnacious, deadpan, like a security guard.

'Have you any means of identification?' he asked.

'No . . . er, not on me. All I've got are these.'

I showed him my receipts from the Salvation Army and Bruce House. He took the letter from the Salvation Army which had referred to me as the 'above-mentioned gentleman', and he told me to sit down with the others and wait.

There were about 150 other men in the room, all facing the same direction, sitting on the same kind of plastic bench seat I had seen in the Spike. Many had the air of men who knew their waiting had only just begun. I took my place behind an ashen-faced Scot with a rucksack, who spoke out of the side of his mouth as though he were telling secrets of national importance. To my right was a stocky man in his thirties who showed me a list of job agencies in Germany.

'I'll telephone as many as I can when I get over there,' he said. 'I think I stand a fair chance of getting work from what I've heard.'

'One agency will play you off against the other,' said the Scot from the corner of his mouth. 'Remember, they've got two million fucking unemployed in Germany, they're hardly going tae give you a plum job when there's Germans out of work.'

'Well, that's not what I've heard,' said my neighbour. 'I've heard you can earn two hundred and fifty quid a week on the building sites, and that's on jobs the Germans won't even touch themselves.'

'You can earn that here,' said the Scot, twisting his mouth even further round his face. 'I was clearing more than two hundred fucking quid a week just washing up fucking pots at Sullen Voe. I did it twice.'

He showed us two oil company identity cards from Sullen Voe, both badly scratched, but clear enough to make out his face in the photograph.

'Why are you in here,' I said, 'if you were earning more than two hundred quid a week?'

'Well,' said the Scot, 'when you've got a few hundred in your pocket, you want to get out and fucking spend, don't you? You cannae spend it on anything at all up there. Anyway, there's plenty of jobs in London.'

The drinking party at the other side of the room near the back was getting rowdy. The 'leader', a tiny red-haired Glaswegian, had just opened another bottle of VP sherry, and was tasting it to make sure it came up to standard. His eyes stayed on an open-mouthed man a few chairs away whose hand was out-stretched, willing his leader to give him the next turn at the bottle. The little Scot took his time, he was in control, the Keeper of the Grog. His hands were huge for such a small man, paws which seemed to grip the bottle as tight as a wrench. He judged that it was time for someone else to take their turn, and he passed the bottle across to the man with the open mouth. His companion seized it with both hands and began to guzzle, tipping the bottle back too far, so that the wine spilled out over his lips.

'None of your fucking tricks,' said the Leader, snatching the bottle back and passing it to a more deserving case. The open-mouthed man followed the movement of the wine with his head, his hands snatching at the air like a baby in a pram.

'But I'm dying for a drink,' he shouted.

The tiny Scot leaped up and grabbed the other by his lapels. He was a good six inches shorter, but his expression left no doubt about who would come off best. He was the lion who could bring down the ox.

'Any more of your fucking tricks, and you're oot,' he shouted, his right hand sweeping a huge arc in front of the bigger man's face. The big man stared at the outstretched finger, as if he had just found it by accident. The Scot resumed his seat, the village tyrant on his throne. He adjusted the rake of his blue cotton hat and resumed command of the bottle.

The Tannoy boomed out my fictional name: 'Tony Crabbe, Box Four, Tony Crabbe.'

It took me a few seconds to react. Even though I had been on the road for more than two weeks, I had rarely been called by anything but my first name.

A man in a tee-shirt sat behind the security screen in Box

Four. I could make out the emblem of a sports-goods firm embroidered on his chest.

'Have you been working since you left Doncaster?' he asked me.

I told him my usual story about helping a friend convert his London house, and then being kicked out.

'What sort of a friend is that?' he said.

'I don't know,' I said.

I told him I had been living on my savings for the past year.

'Don't you like a drink now and then,' he said, 'or some new clothes?'

'I had a drink now and then,' I said.

'All right, wait over there.'

He had been polite, almost sympathetic. I waited for an hour. From the lavatory in the corner came the sound of breaking glass. I had been told that a police station was sited round the corner specifically to deal with the violence and drunkenness in Scarborough Street, and I expected the police would be called at any minute. I watched with apprehension as a tiny man with a pointed beard began to threaten a bruiser with a broken nose. It was a fight which was too close for comfort. In the queue, near the entrance, a man in a shabby grey suit was falling asleep as he stood. He swayed backwards and forwards like an oil derrick, until finally, after two or three minutes, he slumped to the ground in a sitting position. The shock of his fall woke him momentarily, and he dragged himself, nose down, along the floor to a corner where he stretched out full-length among the litter and fell asleep. No one moved to help him; several men stepped over him as though he were a pile of dirty rags.

An Ulsterman crouched in front of me, and took out a can of lager from a plastic bag.

'If only they'd give me more money,' he lamented, 'I'd be able to drink so much more.' He winked at me.

A dark-faced Pole crept up on him from behind, and pretended to search his hair for nits. He uncovered a bald patch, and stood back pointing at it.

'What's this then?' he said.

'Listen,' said the Ulsterman with a twinkle in his eye, 'if it's behind me, I can't see it. And if I can't see it, it doesn't bother me.' He winked at me once more. It was a fraternal greeting, the brotherhood of the drinking classes.

'Tony Crabbe, Box Four, Tony Crabbe.' The Tannoy called me for my third interview.

It was a different man behind the security screen, younger, wearing an open-necked shirt. He was more friendly than the previous two. I asked him if it was possible to get a grant to buy myself some new clothes.

'Well, I'm afraid not,' he said. 'The law states that you have to have a permanent address before any application for clothing can be considered. I think the view is that you might ruin the clothes if you slept rough. It would be different if you booked into a hostel for a week at a time, but at the moment you just wouldn't qualify.'

I was sent back to my seat to wait for another call. A full-scale drinking party was now forming round the Ulsterman. I sat next to a well-scrubbed man who looked like a jolly farmer. At first I thought he looked sober, but it soon became clear that he was very drunk indeed.

'I know Manchester,' he said. 'Is Doncaster anywhere near there?'

'No,' I said, 'it's on the other side of the Pennines.'

'In Yorkshire!' he said as if he had had a sudden flash of intuition. 'Yorkshire's the biggest county in the country, isn't it?'

'Yes,' I said.

He took a quarter-bottle of vodka from the pocket of his tweed jacket and drank deep. The Pole began to worry him for a share, but was refused.

'In Poland,' he said, 'everyone can afford to drink twice as much as us.'

'Well, why don't you go back there if it's so fucking good?' said the Ulsterman, who seemed to be getting less affable with every sip of beer.

I moved away for my own safety, and leaned against the wall near the door. As the drunks grew in numbers, I thought my best course would be to keep as mobile as possible so that I could dodge trouble when it happened. I had been waiting for three hours, and many of the people in the room had arrived before me. I wondered how they could tolerate such long periods of waiting on a regular basis in such unsavoury and dangerous conditions. A small, muscular man who had a conviction for grievous bodily harm approached me. He had been with me in the Spike van two nights before.

'You didn't spend a second night there, then?' he said.

'No, one was enough for me.'

'And me,' he said. 'Mind you, I really enjoyed that shower. That was the only good thing about it. The food was fucking bad though, eh? Worse than the stuff they give you in jail in Northern Ireland.'

I asked him what he thought of the late-night interrogation.

'Well, I don't think they got much from me,' he said. 'I gave them a false name for a start. They asked me if I'd got any tattoos, and I said yes, an eagle on my left forearm and a heart on my right. The stupid buggers didn't even look.'

He rolled up his sleeves to reveal a clover leaf tattooed on his left forearm and a shield and dagger on the right. The Skeleton was skipping from one side of the room to the other by now, apparently terrified for his life. He clutched his Habitat catalogue as though it were his only friend, and I heard him say: 'Oh, they're fighting there, I can't go there. And they're fighting there too.'

'I won't be long in here,' said the man who'd just shown me his tattoos. 'I was in and out of here in an hour last week.'

He told me he had received more than £60 the week before, but I thought it must have been for two weeks' benefit.

'I'll be the next pay-out but one,' he said. 'I've cracked it.'

He was right, he was in the next pay-out but one.

We were joined by a prostitute he knew. She was one of only five women in the room, and she waved to a woman friend with almost identical dyed-blonde hair.

'He's kicked me out,' she said. 'I'm staying with George now, just temporary.'

She was very thin, with poor teeth, and aged somewhere between twenty and thirty-five. Several of the men in the room stared at her legs, and she became more cheerful.

I was called for my final interview. It was to a different cubicle and this time the official was middle-aged and dressed in a sober shirt and tie. He was firm, but polite.

'I'm not trying to call your integrity into question,' he said, 'but how do I know that you are who you say you are? You could call yourself Mickey Mouse if you wanted.'

The game was up. I had known from the start that it was only a matter of time before my identity was called into question. But I had found out what I wanted to know. Scarborough Street was one of the most dangerous and squalid places I had visited as a down-and-out. Yet the staff, behind their barricades, had done their best to treat me as a human being, in spite of their grave suspicions.

But I wondered at the wisdom of segregating the drunks and misfits. Was it enough to say that most of them did not mind the terror of Scarborough Street, because they were participants? I thought of my own fear, and that of the Skeleton who had been less well able to cope, and I could not help thinking that we had both been betrayed.

It was late afternoon, and I looked for a public bath-house where I could have a shave and a leisurely wash. I wanted to be as clean as possible for the following day when I intended to start my serious search for casual work. I was forced to record the loss of my beard on film for continuity reasons, and I dared not risk open filming in one of the hostels. If I were to be discovered as a television reporter, I would be in danger from my fellow down-and-outs.

There was a bath-house I knew in Camden Town where I could hire a bathroom and a towel for 27 pence. It seemed ideal, but I had one more problem. I would have to film there without permission, because the local authority which ran the bath-house also ran one of the hostels I had stayed in, and too many questions might ruin the whole project.

'Have you any single baths?' I asked the girl at the reception desk.

'No,' she said, laughing, 'only doubles. So you and your friend should be all right.'

The friend was Alex, the cameraman, who booked a bathroom separately. We walked along a steamy corridor past a sign which pointed to 'Gentlemen's hot baths'. The temperature rose as we climbed the stairs. We emerged facing a row of single bathrooms which seemed to overhang a swimming pool. I could hear children playing below, but the pool was obscured from view. There seemed to be no attendant on duty, and I chose a bathroom near the centre. There was a large white bath, a chair and a mirror, and Alex began to prepare his camera.

Suddenly a voice said: 'Go and sit down. The notice says sit down and wait for the attendant.'

He was an elderly pugnacious man, a man who knew The Rules. He marched us back to an open space near the staircase. We sat, and waited. A few minutes later, he showed us into separate bathrooms where he had already run hot water. The object of our visit – to film the shaving of my beard – seemed to be slipping from view. I locked my bathroom door, and began to prepare the cheap throwaway razor and the shaving cream which together had cost me about 10 pence. I hoped the attendant would go away. I waited, and waited, but he stayed.

I heard Alex say: 'I've got no soap, can I ask my mate to lend me half of his?'

'Oh, all right,' said the attendant, grumpily. 'But be quick.'

Alex knocked on my door. He entered and quickly took out his camera. He filmed me lathering my face, but I had not had a chance to begin shaving when the attendant began to shout.

'What are you doing in there?' he said.

'We're breaking the soap in two,' said Alex.

'Well, hurry up about it, and get back to your own bathroom,' said the attendant with an understandable edge of panic in his voice. His mind was racing through the possibilities of what might be taking place.

I began to shave.

'Come on, get out!' His voice was hysterical, and Alex found it difficult to carry on filming.

'Open this door,' screamed the attendant, banging on the door. 'I'll fetch the Supervisor.'

It was hopeless. Alex hastily put his camera back in its bag, and we opened the door.

'Right,' said the old man, 'we'll see the Supervisor about this.' He was shaking.

I washed off the shaving cream, and joined Alex in the

Supervisor's office. I felt like a schoolboy caught in possession of smutty pictures and now called to the headmaster's study.

'Now, only one person speak at once,' said the Supervisor, a slim man with the calm of a snake exterminator. 'There's no sense in shouting at each other, or we'll never hear what the other side is saying.'

He listened to the most bizarre catalogue of accusation and counter-accusation like a High Court Judge, a man who knew the Rule Book of the public baths backwards.

Alex said: 'We're just two working blokes, trying to make a fresh start. We just wanted to get cleaned up and have a bit of a chat, and this chap stopped us.'

'Bloody right I stopped you,' said the attendant. 'You'd locked the door.'

The Supervisor paused for a moment before delivering his judgement.

'Bathrooms,' he said with great dignity, 'are for washing in, not for talking in.'

There was a reverent silence.

We left the bath-house and completed our filming in a dingy bathroom owned by the BBC.

The following morning, I asked the Salvation Army in Great Peter Street to help me replace my torn and grubby clothes. The porter on the gate suggested that I try a second-hand clothes shop on the other side of Vauxhall Bridge.

'But I haven't got much money,' I said.

'Oh, well, you'd better wait for the major's wife,' he said. 'She'll be up in a minute.'

She was a motherly woman who looked as though her duties at the hostel prevented her from having much time to herself.

'What size waist are you?' she asked.

'Thirty-two,' I said.

'You look more than that,' she said. 'My son's about your size and he's bigger than a thirty-two. I'll get you a pair of his old trousers.'

The trousers were size 34 and navy blue. I guessed they had been part of her son's Salvation Army uniform. She held them up against me. They were slightly too large.

'They look about right,' she said. 'You can have them for twenty-five pence, all right?'

'Yes,' I said. 'And have you got an old coat I could have?'

She disappeared once more into a back room, where she found a fawn gaberdine coat, styled for an elderly man. I held it up against my body.

'It seems about the right length,' I said. 'I'll take it. How much?'

She ran her fingers through her hair, as if she were embarrassed to think of a price. 'Call it another twenty-five pence,' she said.

Later that day, I changed into all the better-quality clothes I had acquired during my travels: the jacket and shirt from the Simon Community, the tie I had bought for 15 pence at Bruce House, the trousers and coat from the Salvation Army. Strangely, I felt as uncomfortable in them as I had in my tattered coat. I looked like an unsuccessful clerk, a failure of a higher order on the social scale, but a failure nevertheless.

It was Friday night, and the hostels were filling up for the week-end. I tried to book a bed at the old Charing Cross Hospital which was now run as a hostel by the St Mungo charity.

'We've got nothing until next week,' said an upper-class man on the reception desk. 'The only place you'll find a bed in at this time is Bruce House.'

I was dismayed. How, I wondered, would the residents of Bruce House react to my new persona? After all, I would be one of the smartest men in the hostel.

In the television room, sitting among the usual drunks, I felt more isolated than ever. In my new clothes I could no longer blend with the background. I watched an American detective story, trying my best to concentrate on the screen without attracting anyone else's attention. There was a sudden crashing noise from the back of the room, as a heavyweight drunk charged into the room, a harmonica in his hand. He knocked over half the chairs in the back row before coming to rest near the far wall. I looked round to see what was causing all the noise. The drunken man was smiling, pleased with the reaction he had provoked. His eyes scanned the faces in the room, and lighted on mine. A man with a clean-shaven face and a tie was good for some sport, he thought.

'Hey you,' he shouted, 'who are you fucking looking at?'

He walked towards me. I kept glancing back to see where he was. He drew nearer and nearer.

'Hey, you, look at me,' he said. He was almost on top of me, brandishing his harmonica like a weapon. I stood up and dodged past him before he had a chance to land a blow. I walked out into Covent Garden, looking for a pub where I could enjoy a drink without risking attack. I wanted to drink to insulate myself against the depression of staying in Bruce House. It was the first time I had even considered alcohol as an anaesthetic. It became easy to see how a person could slip into alcoholism simply by staying too long in such a place.

It was a pub in Endell Street, a warm family pub with shining brass and happy voices. I bought two pints of bitter, half my day's allowance for food and drink, but it seemed worth it to buy a few hours of warmth in pleasant company. By the time I returned to Bruce House, most of the residents were too drunk or too tired to care who I was, or how I was dressed.

Looking for casual jobs was hard, psychologically wearing work, more tiring than I could have imagined. It was like being dragged around town by your mother when you are too small to understand why. Each extra journey seemed unbearably long, each rebuff a personal affront. It was worse that I desperately wanted to work. I suspected that many of my fellow dossers regarded their casual shifts as a windfall, a bit of extra drinking money, a chore to be endured for the pleasure to come, whereas I wanted the discipline of work, the feeling of worth that I hoped it would bring, the sense of pattern to my life.

I tried six Mayfair hotels in the first day, all of them large and well-known, all equally dismissive. At Claridge's, I was sent to the staff entrance at the back by a uniformed doorman in a tail-coat. He pointed the way with a white-gloved hand.

I was determined not to give up. At the end of the first day, I asked the Welshman for advice.

'You should pick your day,' he said. 'Tuesdays, Thursdays and Fridays are best, that's when the rest of them are down the Social Security.'

I met a man in the washroom of Bruce House that night who told me I would have to turn up an hour early to be sure of getting work.

'I usually go down the May Fair Hotel,' he said. 'They start you at seven, but you've got to be there by six at the latest if you really want a job.'

On Sunday, I gave the zoo a final chance. I ran the two miles to be sure of arriving at nine in the morning, but again I failed to find work. I bought myself a newspaper as consolation. It was the first heavyweight Sunday paper I had seen in three weeks, and I found wars that I had not known were going on, power struggles among politicians of staggering irrelevance, posturing by letter-writers, sublime triviality in the women's pages. The only article which rang true with my hard selfish existence was an article about a family of multi-millionaires who had once bought a peerage and avoided tax by living abroad. That, I thought, was the mirror image of my world.

That night, I decided I could no longer bear the thought of sleeping in sheets which someone else had soiled. I took the dirty sheets from my bed in Bruce House, and discovered beneath the mattress a pair of urine-soaked underpants and a copy of the *General and Municipal Workers Songbook*. On page 57 I read:

> There's a long, long trail a-winding
> Into the land of my dreams,
> Where the nightingales are singing
> And a white moon beams.

I took the dirty sheets downstairs and presented them to the men on the reception desk. I had been warned that they might ask for a bribe, but they replaced them without fuss, and gave me an extra blanket. But they made sure that I knew they were doing me a favour.

'The sheets are only changed once a week,' he said, 'and your bed's not due for a couple of days.'

Even the new sheets were grey, the greyness brought about by long periods of use between washings.

That night, when I had settled into bed, I heard a Liverpudlian's voice complaining loudly.

'You dirty bastards,' he said, 'you ought to be fucking skullnecked. You ought to wear fucking nappies, you great babies.'

I knew what he was complaining about. I had seen it myself: a pool of urine stretching for a yard and a half down the centre of the corridor.

'You'd probably shit yourselves in bed rather than get up,' he shouted to the unseen men in their cubicles. 'Well, just remember this, there's genuine fucking shift workers have to stay in this dump, you dirty bastards.'

I heard him turn to his friend who occupied the cubicle next to his and whisper: 'I'm getting out of this gaff tomorrow, I can't fucking stand this. Can you whiff tha'? Why doesn't someone fucking DO something?'

An hour before dawn. Berkeley Square was deserted but the lights in the Rolls-Royce showroom were still on. I had been up since five o'clock to make sure I got there on time. The May Fair Hotel was described as 'smart' and 'modern' in the hotel guides, a five-star hotel 'popular with both business executives and foreign tourists'. A room for one night cost almost twice my weekly allowance for food and accommodation. I arrived at a quarter to six, an hour and a quarter before the hotel was scheduled to take on its casual workers for that morning. I was first in the queue, but only by ten minutes. By 6.30, there were ten of us, and the timekeeper was worried that the passageway to the staff entrance was being blocked. The queue backed up, forcing a sour-faced man to join the line instead of starting his own separate queue on the other side of the door. Until then, it had been a game of cat-and-mouse which of us was going to claim to be first. We watched a lorry install a large refuse skip into a loading bay at the back of the hotel. An Asian man, wearing overalls, began to sweep the area around it.

'He's a good 'un, him,' said a drunken Scouse. 'He's a fucking Indian, but he's a good 'un.'

A younger man said he had worked in Claridge's the day

before, but did not plan on going back.

'You have to go on a Charles Atlas course to work there,' he said. 'Great fucking copper pans, it's murder.'

At seven o'clock, a man in a suit arrived and pointed to three men – the drunken Scouse, a young Irishman and the sour-faced man who had been my rival for being first in line. Then he said: 'Who was first in the queue?'

I was the last person hired. I gave him my National Insurance number and he sent me downstairs with the others. We changed into overalls in a room not much bigger than a broom cupboard. Already, it seemed stiflingly warm. The drunken Scouse said: 'I'd take off your shirt and jumper, you'll be fried alive.' I followed his advice. The overalls made me feel classless in a way my street clothes never could.

I was assigned to the pastry room. The supervisor introduced me to a young Chinese pastry chef called David, who was under great pressure to make croissants for breakfast.

'Do you know where the coffee shop is?' he asked.

'No.'

'Come, I show you.'

He led me along a steeply raked corridor into a corridor full of pipes and electrical wiring.

'Go along there and up the stairs and ask them how many tray of pastry they want.'

I passed through a lower kitchen where a cook was slicing bacon and ham, up a winding flight of stairs into a smaller kitchen which seemed to be for the preparation of drinks and snacks. A Spaniard in a head waiter's uniform asked me what I wanted.

'How many trays of pastries do you want?' I said.

'Fifteen.'

I relayed this message to David.

'Fifteen trays!' he said. 'Go and ask them again, we've never made fifteen trays. Five at very most.'

I returned to the coffee shop.

'Oh,' said the Spaniard, 'I thought you said how many cakes. Tell him we want five trays of pastries in all.'

David seemed greatly relieved at the news, but the order meant he still had another sixty croissants to make. He busied

158

himself with that while I started washing up a pile of stainless-steel pans and bowls which had been dumped on the floor near the sink.

Michel, the head pastry chef, arrived at about half past seven. He was a squat man in his late thirties, with an open handsome face, a chef who had come up through the brutality of an apprenticeship in a patisserie in France. He now gave orders just as brusque as those he once received. His accent was stage-French, like Inspector Clouseau.

'I wernt you to first mup ze flers of ze refrigerators, zen whan you haff dun zat well, you mup ze flers in ze kitchen, OK?'

I had to take up a tray of croissants first, and I almost walked into the eating area of the coffee shop in my overalls.

'Not in there,' said the head waiter dragging me back. I almost dropped all the croissants on the floor. When I returned to the pastry room it was eight o'clock.

'You go for your breakfust now, I zink,' said Michel.

I was served scrambled egg and bacon by another chef, a fat, red-faced man who asked me how much my watch cost.

'It's cheaper than it looks,' I said.

In the staff canteen, the drunken Scouse and the young Irishman were already tucking in. I helped myself to a cup of tea from the counter and joined them.

'Did you read about Lady Barnett's place being done over while her funeral was on?' said the Scouse, whose speech was still badly slurred. 'It was dossers what done it, you know. Mind you, she bloody deserved what she got.'

'Not to top herself, surely?' said the Irishman.

'Well, perhaps not that,' said the Scouse, 'but she deserved all the publicity and that. I mean she enjoyed thieving. She was a fucking gambler too, you know. And a fucking magistrate. I mean, when you've got all the things she had, you've got to enjoy thieving or you wouldn't fucking do it, would you?'

'You're right,' said the Irishman. 'I mean, we do it for survival not for fucking pleasure.'

I asked the Irishman where he had slept the night before.

'In a graveyard,' he said. 'I was a bit fucking steamed, you know how it is. I just lay down, the first place I come to. Anyway, it wasn't a bad sort of night. But this fucking graveyard was next to a railway line, and a train come past about five o'clock this morning and the whole fucking ground started to shake. Fucking Jesus, I thought my time had come then.'

I told them I had spent the night in Bruce House.

'Christ, that place,' said the Irishman. 'I once had all my fucking clothes stolen from there – well, everything but my vest and pants. They come over the top of the cubicle while I was flaked. I had to borrow some fucking clothes to get out of the place.'

The Scouse said Bruce House had a reputation for murder second to none.

'I heard of a bloke who was carrying five hundred pounds killed in there. Five hundred pounds! He was drunk, of course, asking for it. You know, there's one fella in there that's been mugged about a dozen times. His mates get him drunk, then they jump him – regular as clockwork.'

I sipped my tea; it was luxurious to drink it without sugar. I helped myself to toast from the counter and spread it thickly with margarine and marmalade.

'Of course,' said the Irishman, 'I don't usually have to bother with places like Bruce House. I've got this skip of me own. Hey, did you notice, there's an off-licence straight outside the hotel for when we finish?'

'Yeah,' said the Scouse.

When the Irishman had returned to work, the Scouse turned to me, confidentially.

'Never go for a drink with him,' he said. 'He's a nutter, a head case. Never pays for a drink, and he'll expect you to keep buying all night.'

Sour-Face joined us. He looked into the Scouse's eyes.

'How come you never get a job when you're sober, yet as soon as you're drunk, they give you one?' he said.

I returned to the pastry room after half an hour's break. Already there was a huge stockpile of dirty pots and pans, and I had to work non-stop to clear them. There was now a girl working with Michel and David, a nineteen-year-old catering student called Valerie who looked as though she expected to be scolded at every moment. Michel kept taking her bowls to show her where she was going wrong.

'No, we dunt do eet like zat, we must beat it fast, fast or it won't rise.'

He spoke like her father, and she cringed as though about to receive a punishing blow.

Between the three of them, they produced enough pastries to satisfy the coffee shop and the lunchtime restaurants. It was a formidable achievement, and I was exhausted just trying to keep pace with the washing up. I became very possessive about the area around my sink, and I disliked it intensely when my routine was upset. I had set aside one sink for washing, the other for rinsing. From time to time, both Michel and David dropped dirty pans and utensils in the clean water, forcing me to drain the sink and start again. I did not dare to complain. I knew well that I was too low in the scale of things to have an opinion.

'Ma wife, she eez on a zhury today,' said Michel during a brief lull. 'She 'as to go, uzzerwise she would be fined, you know. Anuzzer woman, she deed not come to ze court, and ze judge ask her where she has been. She say she has been to buy a new coat. So ze judge ask her how much the new coat cost. And she say fifty-nine pounds. So he said . . . er . . . zat is how much I fine you. It is serious, you know.'

The other two made a show of listening to the story. David continued to work. When it was over he said: 'My friend, take those up to the coffee shop on the trolley.'

I wheeled eight desserts up the corridor, taking care to avoid upsetting two jugs of cream at the steepest point. I asked for help in ferrying them along the back corridor, and I and a French student transferred each dish individually. I wondered at the wisdom of allowing a porter like me, who might have been sleeping on the streets the night before, to carry uncovered food in this way. Who was to know what diseases I was carrying?

I was allowed half an hour for lunch – veal fritters and chips with mixed vegetables. The drunken Scouse and I were joined by a full-time member of the hotel staff, a tall, tattooed, big-boned youth who claimed he had serious blood-poisoning. He seemed proud of the fact.

'The doctor says I'll be dead if I carry on drinking and smoking and that. I passed out a few weeks ago, and they thought I'd died. I woke up in hospital with a priest standing over my bed,

161

giving me the last rites. It came as quite a shock.'

The Scouse said he liked working for the May Fair Hotel, it was a good class of establishment.

'All the big nobs stay here, you know,' he said. 'They do. Oh yeah, it's five-star this place, you know. They ring up from America and they say: "Book me into the May Fair." Yeah.'

'Who owns the Metropole?' said the man with blood-poisoning. 'It's Grand Metropolitan, isn't it?'

'No,' said the Scouse with derision, 'it's Lonrho, that is. Angus Ogilvy's one of their directors, you know, married Princess Alexandra. A lot of people said he married her because of her money, but he didn't, you know. He liked the girl. In any case, he was a millionaire before he met her.'

'What would you do if you had a million quid?' said the man with blood-poisoning. 'Because I've thought about this a lot, and I know a lot of people say you wouldn't know what to spend it all on, but I'm sure I could think of something, something really good.'

'Me and him,' said the Scouse pointing at me, 'we'd drink it all away, no bother, wouldn't we?'

'Yeah,' I said.

Suddenly the Scouse got up, and rushed towards the counter, where two women in kitchen overalls were struggling with a heavy cardboard carton. He seized the carton from them, almost collapsing with the weight, and began to manhandle it towards a milk dispensing machine. I realized that the weight was too much for him, and I came to his aid. We pushed the carton into the machine, and the old man closed the door.

'Ta,' he said, breathing heavily. When he sat down he said: 'Not too good at lifting weights. But that should have done us a bit of good. If you get in with the girls behind the counter, they'll sometimes give you something to take out, you know, wrap it up and everything. You've just got to show a bit of willing, you know, help 'em with the dishes when they come out of the machine, that sort of thing. If I were you, I'd help 'em push the trolley with all the dishes on this afternoon. You've got to be sharp.'

I returned from lunch at 12.30, and once again the pans had piled up. David asked me to carry more cakes to the coffee shop.

Michel said: 'Dunt tek ze two on ze sad.'

I did not understand.

'You don't want me to take these two?' I said, pointing to two of the flans.

'I've zhust tulled you,' said Michel, as if I were being perverse.

I loaded the dishes on to the trolley, leaving two cakes on the counter, and I set off down the corridor, expecting Michel to call me back at any moment. The call never came.

At 1.30 there was a lull. Michel returned from the staff canteen with what looked like a school lunch. He opened a can of lager and began to pour it into a glass. I set to work, scraping the baking sheets, wiping each one down with a dry cloth.

'Are you a rich man?' I asked Michel.

He ignored me, and continued to read his newspaper. After a long pause, he said: 'You are a funny man.'

He seemed offended that a kitchen porter should have dared ask him such a personal question. Then he said: 'I dunt sink you hev alwez done zis jub. You hev worked elsewhere, hevn't you?'

'Well, yeah, I suppose so,' I said.

'Hevn't I sin your fess somewhere before?'

'I don't know,' I said, worried that he might have seen me on television.

'You live rund here?'

'Yeah.'

'Ah.'

Valerie returned from her lunch break, and Michel began to question her about her college course. Now that the pressure of the cooking was over, he was less authoritarian, but still fatherly.

'How much do you get a wick, Valerie?' he asked.

'About fifty-nine pounds,' she said, submissively. 'I've got this bedsitter. It costs me sixty pounds a month. I don't go out very much.'

'No discoo dawnsing?' said Michel.

'Well, a bit, sometimes.'

Valerie went about her tasks again, and Michel told me the answer to my earlier question.

'There is not mush diffairance betwin ze wages of a kitchen porter and a pastry chef zees days. Zay do not want a qualified chef, zay want someone who can do ze job of a qualified chef for

163

fifty-nine pounds a week. Zay are ze bosses, we are zhust ze people zay imploy.'

As I left the May Fair at three o'clock that afternoon, the supervisor remembered my name. He showed me the route to the timekeeper's office again, and I collected my first wage packet: £11.44. For the first time in three weeks, I felt rich.

I decided to treat myself to better-class accommodation. I found a bed-and-breakfast hotel in Paddington called the Welcome Inn which advertised its prices at £3 a night.

'You don't get breakfast, not for three pounds a night,' said the girl on the reception desk. 'You can get breakfast just round the corner.'

'Why does it say breakfast then?' I asked.

'Well,' said the girl, looking at a notice above her head, 'we have to keep that up there, anyway. It's closed because we're doing some repairs to the cooker, you see.'

I was given a room sharing with two other men. But when I arrived with my clean linen, I found the room already fully occupied. It meant I had to pay an extra £1.50 for a double room. Unlike the hostels I had grown used to, the hotel took women too, and seemed to cater largely for students. In the corridor, a girl made her way to the bathrooms wearing only a tee-shirt and knickers.

There was a huge helter-skelter installed at the back of the hotel, a tower which housed dozens of self-contained bathrooms, each of a unitary glass-reinforced plastic construction, the toilet, hand-basin and shower moulded from the walls and the floor. It meant that, small as these bathrooms were, I at least had the privacy to wash, but the difference in price between this and the hostels was too great for me to risk staying another night. What would happen, I thought, if I failed to get a casual job? How then could I justify spending £4.50 a night on a place to sleep and wash?

The following evening I had a much worse bargain. I paid £4 to share a room with four other men at a hotel in Bayswater. An

Alsatian dog barked ferociously in the hall, and the man at the reception desk said that I could not have breakfast because I was planning to get up too early.

'Can't you make me up a couple of sandwiches tonight instead?' I asked.

'No,' he said, 'the price is for breakfast only.'

My room was squalid, five beds crowded into a space some 20 feet by 15, with a wash-basin in the corner. I went to bed at nine, but I was woken three times by my room-mates as they switched on the light later in the evening. In the morning, I woke two of them as I dressed in the dark at five o'clock.

I arrived at Claridge's Hotel in Mayfair at a quarter to seven, and once again I was first in the queue.

The timekeeper, an elderly man called Alf, who had a huge Roman nose and a moustache so thin it was barely perceptible, gave me a cup of coffee, brought to special order by a Spanish girl carrying a silver tray.

I counted about five hundred tickets in the racks by the timekeeper's office, many bearing exotic names – Indian, Spanish, Filipino. Some of the workers searched long and hard for their cards in the profusion of names, others swooped down on their cards as they passed, plucking them out with a flourish. A severe woman in a dark blue suit walked straight past the timekeeper without looking to right or left: a woman too important to be paid by the hour.

At about 7.30, a man in a charcoal-grey morning suit approached the clocking-on board from inside the building and began to scrutinize the racks of cards as though he were looking for a missing name. His cuffs were starched and pinched by glistening silver cufflinks, his skin had a kind of incandescence, a plump pink like someone who had been vigorously scrubbed in a hot bath.

By eight o'clock, the queue had grown to fifteen men, and at five minutes past, a lank-haired man in a white coat called four men forward by name, then asked me to join them.

'Right,' he said, turning to the rest, 'no more casuals today. You, Crabbe, follow the rest of them and collect your jacket.'

I pushed my way through the rubber swing doors, and hurried along tiled ramps, round illogically angled corners, until I caught sight of the other casual workers walking in line ahead of me. We were each issued with a green nylon jacket embroidered with the words 'Claridge's Personnel' on the breast pocket.

I was assigned to the plate machine, a conveyor-belt dishwasher which had to be fed a constant diet of freshly scraped silver platters, crockery and cutlery. Behind us was a vast, unruly, old-fashioned kitchen, a place which looked as if it had not had a chance to have a rest for a hundred years, where no one could remember the last time they saw anything that looked new. There were half a dozen of us stacking the plates which had just been sent down for breakfast, and it was clear that we were overmanned. The supervisor took me to one side.

'Go on the plunge,' he said. 'I'll show you where it is.'

I followed him to a small room off the main kitchen where a white-bearded giant in an apron was scrubbing furiously at huge copper pans. He looked like an Old Testament prophet, massively built with grey curly hair.

'Hello,' he said, 'my name's Bernardo . . . actually it's Bernard, but I like the sound of Bernardo better. My girl friend was Italian, from Napoli, and I like Italian wine, Cinzano especially, it's beautiful. I'm glad you've come, I don't know what I'd have done if I'd been left on my own, because it's really been hell in here this morning. Well, the truth is it wouldn't have got done. Can you fill that sink up with hot water?'

He talked non-stop, a conversation with himself that lasted all day. I hardly spoke at all. The slightest word from me would prompt Bernardo into great sermons or maudlin stories of his past, punctuated by shrieks of panic as he imagined himself engulfed in a rising tide of pots and pans.

'In a few minutes,' he kept saying, 'the pots will reach up to here,' and he indicated a height some twelve inches taller than himself. 'You see, up to here.'

But the tide never came, and in the end I was as drained by the emotion of constant and unfulfilled anticipation as much as by the sheer hard work.

Bernardo hated chefs and cockroaches with almost equal vigour.

'If you see a cockroach, crush it with that spoon,' he said.

166

A young chef chided him for using soap on his favourite frying pan.

'Typical,' said Bernardo. 'They don't know what they want. They're idiots all of them. Don't even speak to them, or they'll have you working non-stop.'

He took a long iron hook and walked round the kitchen, gaffing pans by their handles and towing them along the floor of the pot room like reluctant dogs on a leash. Once he had captured a pan, he rescued any tit-bits from inside. His day became a never-ending meal in which dessert preceded main course, and main course was succeeded by *hors d'oeuvres*. I wondered if the rich and famous above stairs could know that, by the timing of their orders, they provided the spontaneous sequence of Bernardo's feast.

A wedding party finished its share of the nuptial cake, and five minutes later, Bernardo was picking the icing off the left-over slices. A resident ordered a joint of rare beef in his suite, and Bernardo polished off the pieces left over in the roasting tin. He ate melon balls followed by mayonnaise, a sip of soup followed by a scoop of custard, a Brussels sprout followed by rich chocolate sauce.

'Here, have a bit, help yourself,' he kept telling me.

From time to time, other kitchen porters appeared at the entrance of the pot room, offering him scraps from the plates or dishes they had been cleaning. He refused nothing. He persuaded me to scrape the remains of bacon fat from a hot tray with crusty French bread, and we set aside a fresh fruit salad for later.

'Don't put the bowl down there,' he said. 'Cockroaches. They stripped the skin off an orange of mine last week.'

He had first worked for Claridge's twenty-five years before, in the days, he said, when they gave the staff best steak for lunch. In those days, he said, the head chef was a tyrant, and he approved wholeheartedly of the brutal way he used to treat his staff.

'He used to sack three chefs a day sometimes if they didn't come up to scratch. He would say, "Leave the premises." I'd sack half the present lot.'

The kitchen Tannoy boomed out the lunchtime orders from about 12.30 onwards, a voice like that of a wrestling referee, one that was determined to make no concessions to menu French.

'Two mooles marinny-air-ah!' shouted the announcer. 'One egg doo-vray-ah!'

I took the pot-hook and went hunting in the kitchen. On the floor I could see live lobsters twitching before being placed in the pot; meat was being sliced with a cleaver; a chef wobbled as he stirred his sauce.

'One steak-ah ta-tarr-ah!' shouted the announcer.

'Is it getting hotter?' said Bernardo, trying to tip a gigantic stockpot into the wastebin single-handed. 'I feel hotter. Do you feel hotter? I bet they've switched off the ventilation so they can have it on upstairs.'

'Two escalopps dee voe-ah!' from the loudspeaker.

'You know that Cole Porter nearly committed suicide?' said Bernardo. 'He was going to five or six parties a week, and suddenly, he couldn't stand it any more. Imagine that, with all those film stars and that, and he couldn't stand it. Would you mind going to five or six parties every week?'

'Well, perhaps one or two,' I said.

'I wouldn't mind it. Those waiters coming round with little things to eat. I'd keep taking a handful. Mind you, I bet they serve dry wine, and I don't like dry wine. I'd say to the waiter, "Bring me a bottle of Cinzano." '

He was a casual worker now, like me, even though he sometimes worked four or five casual shifts a week at Claridge's, he said. He knew he was an alcoholic. His girl friend, Chrissy, had died three years before through drinking too much brandy.

'It was liver-failure,' he said. 'She was a lovely girl. A lot of men wanted to take her away from me. We used to dance together in the street sometimes. Once we were dancing in Portland Place and a Spanish woman stopped us and said she wanted to buy us some wine because she liked to see people dancing. She said it reminded her of home. She went to an off-licence and bought us four bottles of wine, and she invited us back to her place. Well, I told Chrissy I thought she was bent, so we didn't go.'

Bernardo told me he drank up to six bottles of wine at a sitting, a practice which sometimes made him lose his temper. He had been thrown out of a Rowton House at Vauxhall the night before, he said, because he had 'reared up' on a man who complained about his snoring.

Our staff lunch was a grand affair: asparagus soup followed by huge portions of roast pork with sprouts, roast potatoes and gravy. There was a dessert which looked like apple crumble, but I had eaten too much already.

'What's he been telling you?' said a small Scot who had been watching Bernardo and me all morning.

'Everything,' I said.

'The human pig-bin, that's what he is,' said Eddie, from Liverpool. 'I've seen him rooting through bins outside as well. My advice is never follow him into the lavvy, the smell would probably kill you.'

After lunch, Bernardo said: 'I can't understand it. I've lost all my energy. Perhaps I've eaten too much.'

But he set to work as hard as usual. His biggest terror was not overwork but finding himself with nothing to do. It was then he felt exposed, vulnerable, without purpose.

'Look as if you're busy,' he told me, 'otherwise they'll give us another job as well.'

The management paid no attention to our labours. As elsewhere in the kitchen, a good worker was not one who worked conspicuously well, but one who was not seen to slow things down.

We received many visits during the day from the compulsive smokers who hid behind a gigantic pan-scrubbing machine which had not been used for years. A man who looked Chinese kept taking me aside on his many smoking excursions, to warn me of Bernardo's madness.

'He's fucking crazy man,' he said, making the gesture of screwing his forefinger against his temple.

The Bengalis returned from lunch. They were a group, quite separate from the rest of us, who cooked their own food in a corner of the kitchen. It was a segregation that many of the others seemed to favour. I gained the impression that many of the casual workers saw them as a real threat to their livelihoods. After all, they were prepared to work for the same low wages as the rest of us, but they could be relied upon to do so without complaining and without turning up drunk.

'They won't stick in this kind of work for ever, their kind,' said one of my fellow casuals. 'As soon as they've saved up enough money, they'll be off – with a bit of luck.'

We had nearly reached the end of our day's work. Bernardo told me that he was not looking forward to staying in Bruce House that night.

'They shut the windows, and I can't breathe,' he said. 'I lived in a tent for three years in Barnet. I paid this farmer a rent of ten pounds a week, and I made the tent myself. It was a good place to stay. I'd like to do the same sort of thing again if I can save up enough money to buy myself a tent and a sleeping bag. They've got sewn-in groundsheets now.'

He said what he really wanted was a permanent place of his own, a secure room in a house.

'I wouldn't want no furniture or nothing, I'd kip on the floor, I wouldn't mind, but I'd like a room to myself in a house. Nobody would bother about me snoring there. I don't know why they don't let us use all those empty houses. There are more empty houses than there are homeless people, you know, and some of them are empty just because people have got fed up of living there. Well, I wouldn't mind living there.'

At 5.30, we finished work and had our last meal of the day – a massive plate of ravioli and tomato sauce. I had never eaten so well. I went with Bernardo to the timekeeper's office where we were to collect our pay packets, but they had lost all trace of my name.

'Whereabouts did you say you worked?' said the staff manager.

'In the plunge room,' I said. For a moment it looked as though I had worked eight hours for nothing. The supervisor was called and he vouched I had worked there that day. I was handed an envelope containing £12.20.

'Would you stay at Claridge's if you were a millionaire?' asked Bernardo.

'No,' I said, 'a bit too old-fashioned.'

'I'd stay in the Hilton,' he said. 'Very modern there, not like this place. It's got bars and everything – a lot of life. If you were a millionaire and you tried to bring a blonde or something back to your room in Claridge's, they'd say to themselves, "There's something not quite right about that one, let's have him out." Victorians they are.'

*

They called me Yorkie; Yorkie in bed 208. It seemed a cosy enough place to live if you didn't mind the violence and the stench of urine. But I did. And I felt angry that I had been taken in by the high reputation of the charity involved – St Mungo's. By the time I left their hostel, I was in fear not only of the inmates, but of the staff as well.

I arrived at the Old Charing Cross Hospital only an hour after pub opening-time. It was a decaying wedding-cake of a building which stank of stale urine: a heady smell that filled the reception hall like gas. There were drunks to be seen propping up the counter at all times of day, yet that night the man on reception duty seemed sober, correct, almost academic.

I paid him £11.55 for a seven-day stay, a price which included breakfast every day. My bed was in a large room, the whole of one ward of the old hospital. There was a reading lamp casting a cone of light on to bed 208. The man in the bed next to it was already under the covers, as though he were a patient receiving a visitor.

'I apologize for being drunk,' said his guest, a weasel-faced man who was sitting on the bed, 'but hello anyway, whoever you are. I'm skint. Are you going for a drink?'

'I might do, later,' I said.

'Well, will you take me with you?'

'I'm just going to get a bite to eat first, all right?'

There were several men unconscious on their beds as I left. By the time I returned at eleven o'clock the drunks had multiplied five- or six-fold. The stairs leading to my ward were flooded. Had it been a burst pipe, I wondered. Or a bath overflowing from an upper floor. From the basement, I heard the sound of trickling water, and I looked down the lift-shaft in the stairwell. A drunken man appeared, lurching his way up the stairs. The flood was urine. It cascaded down every step, a thin tide of fetid liquid which the residents paddled through on their way to bed.

'You need fucking wellies in this place,' said a man coming down the stairs.

'Isn't there a toilet?' I asked.

He stopped, thinking hard.

'Oh, there is one. I think the nearest is way past reception. Go back to the ground floor, turn right past reception, along a corridor, turn right, up some stairs, and it's somewhere down that corridor on your right.'

How could people live like this, I thought, as I picked my way up the stairs, keeping to the edges where the puddles were fewest. Why did the people in charge do nothing about it? Even buckets on each landing would have been a help.

'Hiya, Yorkie,' said the invalid in the next bed to mine. He had a different visitor this time – a drunken caterer from the Inns of Court, who looked like a plain-clothes policeman, apart from the eyes.

'Whisky's what the barristers have,' he said. 'Bottles of the stuff . . . and port, and brandy. And when they get together for a fucking meal, you wouldn't believe the amount they spend on booze. They think nothing of drinking two bottles each. And we're not talking about cheap stuff now, fucking seventeen quid a throw.'

He regaled us with tales of barristers' drinking bouts, in which the officers of the court were seen to dance on tables or slump unconscious to the floor. It was a parable designed to show not so much the dangers of drink, as its universal appeal. I was being invited to feel envy for Queen's Counsel, because they could afford to drink more and better booze than me.

In the centre of the room, an Ulsterman with a face like a chow dog began a threatening dance, shouting, abusing, telling us all he was going to give someone a good thumping.

'You've chosen the right fucking end to stay, anyway,' said the Caterer. 'That fucker wouldn't dare come down this end. Straight out of the fucking window – and he knows it.'

The Ulsterman seized on this invitation and turned towards us.

'All right, you bastard, come here and tell me what you just fucking said.'

'Get back to your fucking end, or we'll have you,' said the Caterer.

'No fucking chance, sonny, I'll kill yous bastards first.'

The Caterer walked towards him, and the two men seized each other by their shirts. I decided to leave before the fight started.

'I know you, cunt,' said the Hard Man, as I passed. 'I've met you before, you fucking bastard. You'll be next.'

I brushed past him. He seemed far too drunk to do any harm. By the time I had returned from the lavatories, the fight was in full progress, and the Hard Man seemed to be getting the worst of it. He had dragged a stocky Englishman out of bed, and his assailant, dressed only in his underpants, was trying to wrestle him to the ground. The Hard Man punched and kicked, lashing out wildly, forcing the other man to defend himself blow for blow. In the half-light of the bedside lamps the fight took on a surreal quality as the two men, one a dark-clothed figure, the other white-skinned and naked, dodged in and out of the shadows.

The Hard Man kicked his opponent over my bed, sending the mattress and all the bedding slithering to the floor. The kicking and punching continued for several more minutes, the stocky man apparently getting the better of the bare-knuckle contest. I could see blood pouring from the Ulsterman's left eye as he was pushed to the ground.

'Right, now give up,' said the naked man.

'Fuck off, you English bastard,' said the Hard Man, his head in a neck-lock. A small puddle of blood was caught on his lower lid.

'Now calm down,' I said, realizing that the fight was over, and that the Hard Man was powerless. 'Just get cleaned up and go to bed.'

'You fucking cunt, I'll kill you next,' he said struggling. The white of his left eye had turned a dull red.

'Calm down,' I said. 'It's all over. Just get cleaned up and go to bed. All any of us wants is to go to bed.'

'My fucking mates'll see to yous bastards, you see if they don't,' said the Hard Man.

I remade my bed, and undressed. As I lay there, I looked down the ward and wondered if the Hard Man was serious about his mates coming later. I could not sleep and, for an hour, I turned restlessly in my bed.

They arrived at about one in the morning, two men sober enough to do a lot of damage. I held my breath.

'Right, you, cunt, get out,' said one, standing over the naked Englishman's bed.

'Hold on, mate,' said the man in the bed. 'Let me just tell you how it happened.'

To my surprise, they allowed him to tell his side of the story. One of them did not believe it and moved forward to drag the man out of bed.

'It's right what he's telling you,' I said from the safety of the darkness. They both stopped and turned round. There was a pause, then one of the men said to his friend: 'OK, let's leave him.'

By some miracle, the judgement had gone against a further beating. It had been as chancy as the flip of a coin.

Breakfast was served in the foul-smelling basement the following morning. By the time I reached the kitchen I did not feel hungry. In the face of this squalor, the breakfast was good, hot and well-prepared, and I could not understand how a hostel could be so inconsistent.

I sat beside a pale old man who was finishing the last clues of that morning's *Daily Telegraph* crossword.

'I don't think the first part of the clue was germane to the solution at all,' he said.

Two teenage youths came in. One, tall and gormless, seemed to be trying to make as much noise as he could.

'Oh, I do dislike that one,' said the frail old man. 'He started throwing food about everywhere yesterday. It's very distressing.'

Violence started at eleven o'clock the following night. I was assaulted by a man from reception who followed me into the toilets as I arrived. He was lurching-drunk, goggle-eyed and belching as he pushed up against me by the urinal.

'Where's your fucking ticket?' he said.

'Who are you?' I asked, fearing he wanted to steal it.

'Never mind who I fucking am, show me your ticket, come on.'

'Look, mate, I've only got two hands, and I'm holding a bag and a radio in one of them.'

I showed him the ticket, holding tightly on to it as he focused on the print.

'Right,' he said, apparently approving what he saw.

'Now you tell me who you are,' I said. 'Are you from reception?'

'I've told you, never mind who I fucking am,' he said, following me out of the lavatory. In the corridor he began jostling me again, as if he were escorting me off the premises.

'Stop that!' I said, 'Stop assaulting me.'

'I just want to check your ticket,' he said, 'show me your ticket.'

He was a heavy man, and he was becoming very aggressive. I

appealed to the crowd round the reception desk for help.

'Will someone stop this man assaulting me,' I said. 'He's already checked my ticket, but he won't tell me who he is.'

The fat man lunged towards me, but he was held back by four others.

Someone said: 'Put that knife away.'

I did not wait to see who had the knife. I ran up the stairs, along the corridor, through the double doors leading to my ward, and to safety.

A love-song was drifting across the still air, a soft sad lament of a lover left alone. It was Sam, the West African, whose bed was next to mine.

'Ain't got money,' he sang, 'got no multi-colour house. I got none, you got two. But I got something, which you ain't got, babe, I got love for you, you never buy, baby . . .'

It was a song of a poor boy left alone by a rich girl, of money coming before love, and, for a moment, the men lying on their beds had gone quiet. One put down the girlie magazine he had been reading, another lay down and closed his eyes. I stood, listening, regaining my breath.

The music was interrupted by the flash of a torch at the far end of the room. A short dark man with a pencil moustache walked softly up to the Caterer and snatched a bottle from his hand. He asked if everyone was booked in. We told him we were.

'If when I have to come up here again, and I hear any noise at all,' said the man with the torch, 'you're all going to have to be booked out instantennanous.' He sounded drunk.

'Where were you last night?' I said. 'There was a lot of violence going on.'

'If you've got some complaint to make, come doon and make it,' he said.

I followed him downstairs to the reception desk, where a number of drunks were shouting. The man who had assaulted me seemed to have gone. The man with the torch introduced me to his colleague, a fat man with a pen, his fellow supervisor.

'It's a bit late to complain about last night innit?' he said.

I told them both about the violence of the night before, and I asked why, if they were so noise-conscious, they had not stopped it.

'Nobody informed us,' said the fat man.

'Can't you hear?' I said. 'The noise must have travelled right through the building.'

'What, down here? Very rarely.'

The man with the torch said: 'Do you think it's reasonable if we put our lives on the line?'

'Why didn't you call the police?' I said.

'Well, why did no one else complain about it?' he said.

I gave up. I thought back to the Salvation Army and how quick the staff had been to stop violence when it started. I tried another tack.

'Why do you let people urinate on the stairs?' I said.

'What do you expect me to do?' said the fat man. 'Go round and tie a knot in it or something?'

The cardboard boxes had been out in Mortimer Street since eight that evening; five of them evenly spaced along the pavement. Two had the labels of Italian refrigerator manufacturers printed across them; one bore the name of a Japanese electronics firm. They were large boxes, substantial enough to withstand a journey across several continents, and now they had reached their final destination: as temporary housing for the jobless in the capital city of the United Kingdom.

The men inside were warm and judiciously drunk. Their boxes were the first in the queue, and they had every reason to sleep easy. Tomorrow they would be first in line for the pick of the casual jobs. If they were lucky, they would earn a full £11 for an eight-hour day in the heat of some backstreet kitchen in Soho or Kensington. But, for that privilege, they would first have to brave the cold of the night.

By four in the morning, the queue outside the government employment agency in Mortimer Street had grown to about a dozen men. The newcomers were not drunk enough to sleep on the cold pavement, nor were they sober enough to have booked into a hostel in time. They stood in a limbo between inebriety and sobriety, whiling the night away.

'The only thing that kept me at that place was the chef,' said a small Jew who looked like a hamster. 'He gave me glasses of wine.'

A tall man with a posh voice emerged from one of the cardboard boxes, and said he was going to look for a cup of tea. He tucked a scarf down his neck and set off.

'You know,' said the Hamster, 'you could open a stall, and I reckon you could sell cups of tea at eight pence a cup and make a profit. I bet you'd have people queueing up.'

A young Liverpudlian, who wore his home team's football scarf, said he was not enthusiastic about politicians.

'None of them are any good,' he said. 'Jim Callaghan wasn't very good, he was getting a bore, like.'

'Heath was about the best, I think,' said the Hamster. 'Don't you think Heath was all right?'

'He had some good ideas, like, Edward Heath. But it's like everything with the Conservatives, like, the working class don't get a chance. They'll stop you some way.'

The Hamster did not seem impressed, and the Liverpool supporter pressed his point home.

'Thatcher . . . you've got to get her out because she's making a mess of the country,' he said. 'It's incredible over the last year how many's unemployed, like. Two million five hundred thousand or something. I don't think she can last after the winter personally.'

The man from the cardboard box returned with three cups of tea, two for his friends. He gave one to a small man who was sitting on an upturned milk crate.

'You'll be looking for something more regular, won't you?' said the small man.

'Well, I've just finished not long ago with a firm of bakers down Gray's Inn Road. This is not my line of country, but I do it.'

'Are you a baker?' said the man on the crate.

'No, no, on KP.'

He was a kitchen porter, like I had been at the May Fair and at Claridge's.

'I've had seven interviews,' said the small man, 'but you know how it is, they're very particular when there's not much work around.'

Many of the men in the line surprised me by their respectability. There were several who looked as if they had drunk nothing alcoholic for a long time, and the Liverpool supporter told me he did not drink at all.

'It's just a habit, like smoking,' he said. 'I don't smoke either, or gamble. I don't see the point of it, like, gambling, not unless you're a professional gambler.'

'Joe Coral's a professional, but he backs winners all the time,' said the Hamster. 'He backs you.'

Why were they prepared to queue all night, I wondered, to get the chance of a miserable casual job the following day? I supposed that my experience of being the only man in the line to get a job at both Claridge's and the May Fair Hotel without having my face known, was the problem they faced every week. At least Mortimer Street offered certainty. But for what reward?

'If you do a casual, I can't see the point in declaring it,' said the Liverpool supporter. 'Because, then, what's the point of doing it? If your money's docked off, you're working for nothing, aren't you?'

'I don't know how much you're allowed to earn,' said a red-faced Cockney.

'Twenty-two pounds,' said the Liverpool supporter.

'The best thing to do is, when they ask you to sign, sign a different name,' said a raddled Glaswegian who had been sipping from a quarter-bottle of whisky. 'Don't worry about what name's on the card. Fucking white card, that's just a piece of fucking writing, that's all. You've a fucking job to understand what's on the white card, never mind your name. For educated people, they're as poor a writers as I've ever seen.'

At 4.35, the refuse truck arrived, and men with brooms began to kick the occupants of the boxes awake.

'Come on, time to get up,' said one of the council workmen for the third time. He kicked the box again. Still no movement, and he left the box alone. One by one they woke, some, like wraiths from the tomb, slowly unravelling the blankets swathed about their heads, pale faces blinking at the street lights, shivering against the sudden, sober cold.

The council men dragged the boxes away, loading them into the jaws of the truck, feeding the revolving teeth which crushed them and swallowed them into the vehicle's belly. Then they began to sweep the litter – beer cans, bottles, newspapers, paper cups. The truck drove away.

Deprived of his cardboard box, a man in a grey suit swayed with fatigue, his body convulsed against the cold, the morning air nipping him like a small vicious dog. He leaned against the shoulder of the man in front and fell asleep.

'Lie him down,' said a man to his right.

He was helped to the ground, gradually, where he curled up tight, his eyes closed, still shivering. After a few minutes, his body relaxed.

The gruff Glaswegian said: 'He must've had a good drink last night to be lying there now.'

'Unless he's dead,' said another.

'No,' said the Glaswegian, 'I saw him move.'

At a quarter past six, the wide-boys arrived. They were mostly young and well-dressed and they made no pretence of standing in the queue. They stood at the other side of the door, facing us, daring us to complain.

'What do you think we are, fucking eejits altogether, some o' yous?' said an old Irishman near me.

'We was here yesterday about this time,' said the red-faced Cockney, 'and they was pushing and shoving and fighting, kicking. By the time everyone had pushed in and that, we ended up on the third page. We didn't even get a job even though we was here early.'

A quiet man sidled up to me and stood there, hoping to blend in with the queue. He was a master of his art, submissive, silent with a look of belonging. Within twenty minutes he was established with the rest of us.

Towards the front, the men began to squash closer, pressing up against the office door to prevent the parvenus getting a toe-hold. There were only a few minutes to go.

The civil servant arrived with his book at a quarter to seven. We could see him through the glass of the office door. He did not attempt to come out. One by one the men in the scrummage pushed their government documents through a letterbox, and the official entered their names in his book, issuing them with addresses of the jobs they had to go to that day.

He seemed to favour the late-comers almost as much as those in the legitimate line, which caused the violent pushing to intensify. Some of the men who had been allocated jobs found themselves trapped against the door in the crush, fighting for breath.

A group of women arrived last of all, and walked calmly to the front. No one objected too much – women were a special case. I saw many of the men leaving in triumph – they had been allocated a job which would give them a full eight hours' work. It was what they had prayed for. No one wanted pub work for a mere five hours: that only paid £6 or £7, and table clearing brought in even less.

I heard two men talking about one employer who encouraged casual workers to take thirteen-week contracts. If they worked well, they would be offered permanent jobs.

'Yeah,' said one man, 'but thirteen weeks. Fancy being tied down to that. I mean, if you get bevvied one night, you'd have to turn up the following day or they'd ask questions.'

'No, you wouldn't,' said the other. 'You'd do what the rest of them do – phone up and tell 'em you're sick!'

After the traumas of the past few weeks, Arlington House had the shock of normality. It was almost like booking into a hotel, and I could hardly believe my luck. I was given my own room, with a key, for £13.30 a week. It was the last one vacant, and there were a dozen men in the queue behind me who wanted it.

It was, and still is, the biggest hostel in the country, with more than 1,000 beds, a fact which surprised me since it felt far smaller than many of the other institutions I had recently stayed in. I wandered around downstairs; there were no drinking parties, no discarded bottles, and the air smelt sweet. In the cafeteria, the knifes and forks were made of metal, and the tables were clean.

My room did not look much: a wood-walled cell some 7 by 5 feet. I tried to stretch my arms across it, but it was too narrow. I didn't care. I felt like shouting for joy that at last, at long last, I had a place of my own. It was somewhere I could hang my shirts and my socks to dry, somewhere I could sit and read or write, somewhere from which I could shut the drunks and the psychopaths out, and, amazingly, somewhere I could afford.

The bed had a heavy black metal frame and a blue and white counterpane patterned with diamonds. The laundered pillows bore the words, 'Rowton Services Ltd'. It was a commercial concern! It seemed to me remarkable that a company could offer such facilities for profit, when the local authority had offered far less.

There was a cupboard above the bed with enough room inside for shirts and jackets, and three shelves for socks and other odds and ends.

I put down my bag on the wooden chair by the bed, and realized that I would at last be able to walk freely without it. I would be able to leave my coat in my room, too, and watch television downstairs in my shirt sleeves if I felt like it.

I walked through the front entrance into the cold open air, and then returned; just to feel the sensation of being able to come and go as I pleased. No turnstiles, no men pestering me for my ticket, just a key in my pocket. I had found a home, at last.

Out of curiosity, I wondered if it was possible to find a home more permanent still than Arlington House. The council official in Westminster was friendly, but his message was clear: there would be no possibility of a council flat for a long time.

'I should think it would be a year at least before you go on the active list,' he said. 'There's so many single people involved, we're in a sort of vague bit of trouble here, you know. People say: have you got any old derelict houses that we can sort of do up, or move into and do up ourselves? They're gone, they've all been snapped up.'

The flats advertised in the newspapers were well out of the range of my weekly allowance and required large deposits of money.

I went to a lonely gatehouse outside Euston Station where a group of charity workers ran a service called 'Alone in London'. They offered me information about hostels which was hopelessly out of date and based on hearsay. They recommended St Mungo's.

'Do you know Arlington House?' said the precious young man who helped me. 'I don't know it, you see.'

He told me the rent was £8.20 a week to stay there – £5 less than the real sum. He advised me to think of squatting, and about getting myself a permanent job.

'If there is anything available,' he said, 'it's going to go to people who are in full-time work.'

I did not know what I thought of squatting. Some of the men I had met in the hostels said they had stayed in squats, but usually not for long. Like so many other things, a squat was a tie, a limitation on freedom.

The Advisory Service for Squatters was badly housed itself: a mean room with a two-bar electric fire, overlooking the Balls Pond Road in London's East End. The walls were covered with posters advertising rock concerts and charting the progress of the Housing Acts. There was a Harrods bag on a table.

'You see, it's not a very good idea to squat, because you need to keep someone in the house all the time during working hours,' said the serious girl who dispensed the advice. 'If you're prepared to do that, especially for the first few weeks, then fine, go ahead.'

It seemed hopelessly impractical, and I was not sure about the ethics of breaking in.

'If you do any damage when you're getting in, you should repair it quickly,' she said. 'Like, if there's a padlock on the door, it's a good idea, if you saw away the padlock, to get another one that looks the same and use it as a lock.'

She gave me a list of addresses of buildings that might be empty, but I still could not reconcile in my mind the notion that I should live in someone else's house for nothing. Because I had suffered so much discomfort in my weeks on the road, I felt I needed to pay.

There was a market near Arlington House. It was my last Saturday on the road. At one end were the fruit and vegetable stalls, at the other, the second-hand carts laden with bric-à-brac of all kinds. Two barrow-boys began to play football with an orange. I watched an old lady rooting through the goods on the poorest of the second-hand goods carts – a collection of items so disparate, it seemed difficult to explain why some of them had been selected for sale at all. There was a plastic bath-rack, still stained with soap; old coat hangers, some of them broken; cups without saucers; cardboard boxes full of old clothes. The old woman spent a long time sorting through the junk, looking for bargains for their own sake. I marvelled at her patience. For all my careful daily budgeting, I knew I was still the rich kid playing at being poor.

Sunday was a day of rest at Arlington House in the most literal sense. It was the only day of the week when the residents were allowed to lie in.

'They don't even ring the bell,' said one of my near neighbours.

Sunday was also the day I washed my underwear for the first time in twenty-six days. Somehow I did not mind the smell, and I scrubbed the garments for an hour to make sure I had rid myself of every last grain of dirt. I put my underpants on the hot-water pipe in my room to dry. I had no change of underclothes, and so I wrapped up well for my morning walk.

In Regent's Park, an elderly couple sat on a bench swaddled in huge blankets, and a woman in a track-suit jogged past so slowly it looked as though the cold had frozen her limbs into slow-motion. I walked along the Regent's Canal, where an angler was pulling out a keep net almost twice his size. An old woman painted a view of a bridge, urged on by her husband, who sat at her elbow, urging her on like a football coach.

There was a lock gate ahead, and I saw a crowd of fashionable people in a gateway. Most did not stay to look at the water, and I wondered what attracted them away. I approached the gateway and suddenly found myself surrounded by crowds, hundreds of people gathered for a Sunday market at Camden Lock. Stalls were selling jewellery, old typewriters, pottery, knitwear. A punk girl with purple hair held a dowdy knitted twinset against herself for size. I felt trapped, I had no right to be there, and I pressed my way through the crowds. On the main road I passed a group of teenaged girls dressed in jumble-sale clothes like my own. Only their clothes were not like mine – decked out with jewellery and badges, they were the height of chic. They giggled when I passed by in my clumpy shoes and wide-bottomed trousers. I was on the right lines, they thought, but I could try a little harder.

'Thanks be to God for His unspeakable gift,' said the sign on the wall of the London Embankment Mission. The gift was a sausage roll of dubious meat content, a plate of instant mashed potato and a cup of sweet tea, and every one of the 115 men in the Gospel Hall knew the quickest way to get it.

This was to be my Last Supper before I returned to my normal life. I watched with interest as the hungriest of God's children took the left-hand aisle. They sat, cheek-by-jowl, hymnbooks in hand, ragged men ready to receive The Word. The centre aisle was populated by those who had learned to control their hunger and thirst after righteousness; there were notably more empty spaces. The right-hand aisle had more empty chairs than full ones. It was the order of things at the London Embankment Mission.

The man in the chair next to mine was a gourmet, a connoisseur of God's gifts, even though they sometimes came from surprising sources.

'You ought to have seen last night's supper,' he said. 'A portion of beans that size, and a fucking egg – in the jail.'

He was a man I recognized from under the Charing Cross Arches, a squashed-faced Glaswegian who carried a carrier bag full to bursting with jumble-sale sweaters.

'Monday, Wednesday and Friday, there's hand-oots here,' he said, 'but Tuesday's a difficult fucking day. Not much going at a' on a Tuesday.'

He said he was heading straight for Charing Cross after the food hand-out at the Mission, so he could catch the first soup van of the evening.

'Good evening, boys,' said a man in a suit at the lectern in front. 'The preacher has not arrived yet, but we'll assume that he will come. Until then, we start by singing this lovely hymn. No. 47, "To God be the Glory".'

The organ began to play, and after listening to the tune, we all began to sing.

> 'To God be the Glory
> Great things He hath done . . .'

The Glaswegian's voice was deep and loud, but he was drowned by a member of the mission at the back, who stood like a rooster on a perch, straining his face towards the ceiling.

> 'Praise the Lord, praise the Lord,
> Let the Earth hear His voice . . .'

The balding man stood before us to lead the prayers. He was not the appointed preacher, and his words came clumsily.

'Lord, we pray that even here, in this little hole here away, in this street from the busy road, you'll come to us, and you'll minister to us, oh gracious Lord. Oh Lord of Light, that you shall come with a

184

meaning with a capital M, to the glory and honour of your Holy Name. Amen.'

The starveling congregation looked up from their prayers, bracing themselves for the amateur sermon that was to be preached in the absence of the main preacher.

The text was the nineteenth chapter of I Kings, the story of how Elijah had killed the prophets, and how Jezebel swore her revenge. I could not follow the moral he drew from the tale.

'He was running away from God,' he told us. 'And maybe in this meeting tonight there is somebody, who's a backslider, and are running away from God. They're running away from something, maybe from their wife, maybe from their children, maybe from the police, maybe from something. They're running away, and yet you're eating the fruit, you're wearing the clothes, you're getting the money, and it's all God's money, and it's all God's fruit, and it's all God's clothes.'

I began to feel guilty. I looked around the audience to see if anyone else had felt their conscience pricked. In the left-hand aisle the hungriest of God's children were all staring at the ceiling. I followed their gaze and saw a sparrow perched high on one of the fluorescent lights above us. It hopped from one foot to the other to avoid the heat of the glass below. Then it flew to the other side of the room, the eyes of half the congregation upon it.

'Sinner, friend,' said the preacher, 'I'm speaking to you tonight. Now it's you I'm speaking to, Sinner!'

The bird flew towards the preacher, circling his head.

'Under the Dominion of Satan and Sin, all the way to Hell, I'm speaking to you now.'

The bird landed once more on the fluorescent light, and settled for a few moments.

'You've wandered for years and years in the cesspool of sin and iniquity,' shouted the preacher, trying his best to ignore the bird. 'You have wallowed in it right up to the neck. And you are just one step from passing from time, into a lost Eternity.'

The sermon came to a rapid end. Even God and hellfire could not compete with the sparrow.

'And now,' said the preacher, 'in the usual manner, we have provided food and drink for you tonight, so if you will kindly make your way to the back of the hall to receive God's gift to you, starting as usual from the aisle to my right . . .'

It was almost a sprint start. The halt and the lame took up their plastic carrier-bags and dashed to the back of the room. At a hatchway, they grabbed plates of mashed potato and a sausage roll, and carried them together with a cup of sweet tea back to their seats. By the time I had followed suit, most of the hungriest of God's children had finished their meal and were ready to leave.

Only the sparrow went hungry that night.

My last morning at Arlington House was an anti-climax. I had expected the transition back to the world of friends and comparative wealth to be dramatic. But I had already crossed half-way over no-man's-land by finding a tolerable place to live. It was true that I still had not found myself a job, and that if my life on the streets had continued, I would have been condemned to casual work for many more weeks, if not months. But I had regained an optimism I had never thought possible at the depths of my short career as a dosser. Of course, my ordeal was soon to end, so I had every reason to feel optimistic. But how long would it have been, I thought, before even Arlington House had seemed a prison? After all, I was bounded by rules which forbade visitors and forced me out of my room during the day. If I remained out of work, those rules, too, would have become a hardship. And how long would I have tolerated the petty restrictions, such as the television being turned off at eleven o'clock, even though I had been watching a programme? Even the best-regulated hostel was still a hostel.

The old Irishman who sat opposite me at breakfast wore a Remembrance Day poppy in his lapel, and murmured poetry to himself.

'Upon the border of that lake's a wood,' he said. 'Now all dry sticks under a wintry sun . . .'

I watched as he poured tea on to his breakfast plate, a trickle at a time, mopping it up with his bread.

'At sudden thunder of the mounting swan,' he continued, 'I turned about and looked where branches break/The glittering reaches of the flooded lake.'

I knew the poem. It was Yeats's 'Coole Park and Ballylee'.

'They're good words,' I said.

He looked up from his plate, a piece of sodden bread in his hand.

'We were the last romantics,' he said, quoting again from the poem. He continued to eat his bread.

I went to my room for the last time. For all its smallness, it had a kind of perfection, an economy. I felt I owed the room a lot, and I sat down to draw a picture of it. It was a kind of tribute.

The door opened.

'Nine o'clock,' said the porter.

I put my drawing hastily away and got ready to leave.

Outside, it was bitterly cold, and I felt my cheeks go smooth in the wind as I stepped into the street. I walked through Regent's Park, a route I had taken many times in the past few days. What, I wondered, had I learnt from my experiences of the past month? I had learned, I thought, that the Welfare State worked, but only after a fashion. It kept the poor alive, but it did little for their spirits.

Was it enough, I wondered, to condemn people to the mean existence of Bruce House without offering them an alternative? It seemed to me ironic that the one place I had found with decent, cheap accommodation was a commercially run hostel which had been making profits long before the Welfare State was thought of.

It seemed to me, also, that the charities and the local authorities which ran hostels were subject to virtually no public scrutiny. Some of them had been able to get away with bad management and inhumanity because the public did not know and did not care. And who was to take the word of a dosser, anyway? I recalled the locked fire doors at Bruce House, and the assurances from the local authority that the practice had already ceased long before my visit. I could not comprehend the minds of men who risked other people's lives for their administrative convenience.

It was true that some of the inmates of the hostels connived at their own squalor, fouling their nests wherever they were allowed. I had despised such people. But the hostels were not simply dumping-grounds for the hopeless cases. Others suffered too. I recalled the Liverpudlian who complained so bitterly about the urine outside his cubicle door. He could afford to move on. But how many thousands like him might find themselves out of work and living in Bruce House without the money to move somewhere better?

It still astonished me that I should have taken to drink myself. Admittedly, I had not drunk much, I had not had the money. Yet, that I should drink alcohol as an anaesthetic to insulate myself from the squalor around me, made me wonder how long Tony Crabbe, had he been fact, not fiction, would have lasted without becoming an alcoholic.

I passed by the aviary at the zoo, the vast cage silhouetted against the morning sky. A huge bird took off from a tree inside, and flew up into the roof and along. Another bird joined it, flying alongside, a smaller bird that looked like a gull. Their wings flapped in unison for a few seconds, then the large bird plunged down into the depths of the cage, while the gull flew on. It had been an illusion. Both creatures had looked as though they were inside the cage, but one had been free all the time.

I walked on, thinking back to the Spike and to the absurdity of an institution which seemed to want to punish the poor for being destitute. How, I wondered, could the destitute be punished more than they were already punishing themselves? And what was the point of maintaining such a vast expensive institution if its aim was to deter people from staying. Why not close it down instead?

I plunged my hands deep in my pockets and headed out of the park towards the city centre. I felt that I needed the warmth of people around me, and I decided to make for a department store, any store, where I could be warm and safe and anonymous. I was due to have a medical that afternoon. I had lost half a stone in weight, but my health did not worry me. I could still not answer the central question: why do men, and a very few women, choose to be dossers?

Perhaps, I thought, because they do not choose at all.

If you would like a copy of our current catalogue please
write to us at:

Quartet Books Ltd
27/9 Goodge Street
London W1P 1FD